OGILVIE'S

BOOK FOR A COOK

A SELECTION OF RECIPES AND OTHER
THINGS ADAPTED TO THE NEEDS OF
THE AVERAGE HOUSEKEEPER,
SOME ENTIRELY NEW, AND
ALL HAVE BEEN
THOROUGHLY
TESTED

OGILVIE
MONTREAL, CANADA
1905

PRINTED IN CANADA

NATIONAL LIBRARY OF CANADA CATALOGUING IN PUBLICATION DATA
Ogilvie's book for a cook / historical notes by Elizabeth Driver.

(Classic Canadian cookbook series)
Includes index.
ISBN 1-55285-504-X

1. Cookery. I. Ogilvie Flour Mills Company. II. Title: Book for a cook.
III. Series.
TX715.6.O45 2003   641.5   C2003-911059-1

The publisher acknowledges the support of the Canada Council for the
Arts and the Cultural Services Branch of the Government of British
Columbia for our publishing program. We acknowledge the financial
support of the Government of Canada through the Book Publishing
Industry Development Program for our publishing activities.

Please note that the ingredients, methods and cooking times listed
in this book are consistent with the kitchen appliances and tech-
niques that were in use in 1905. Current equipment and supplies
may produce different results that are inconsistent with contem-
porary food safety theories.

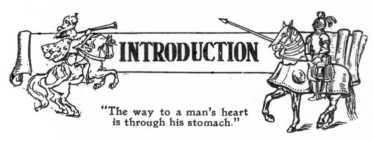

INTRODUCTION

"The way to a man's heart
is through his stomach."

THE OGILVIE FLOUR MILLS CO., LTD.,
after a careful study of the needs of the home-bakers, decided to make a flour particularly suited to their requirements. The result was ROYAL HOUSEHOLD, so named because it is used by the Royal family.

This flour is carefully milled from the very choicest wheat grown in Canada, and each day's milling is subjected to a practical baking test before it is allowed to be given out to the consumer.

Every pound of it is guaranteed, and is especially adapted for either bread or pastry.

The recipes herein presented have been TRIED, TESTED and PROVED. They are not offered as a general cook book, nor as a guide to experts, but simply as a help to the average housekeeper in the hope that it will make easier her search after a variety of good things without calling too much upon her means.

OUR MOTTO:
Highest quality consistent with strict uniformity.

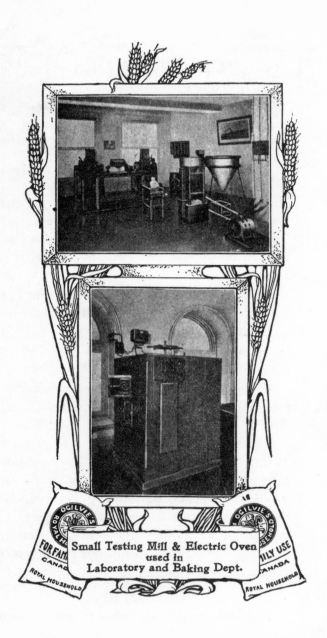

Small Testing Mill & Electric Oven
used in
Laboratory and Baking Dept.

CORRESPONDENCE

If good results are possible, why poor?
I would help others out of a fellow feeling.
—Burton.

FAILURE and disappointment often confront the young and inexperienced housekeeper (and sometimes the experienced one as well) through the misunderstanding or omission of some little detail in preparation. The following recipes have been thoroughly tested, wherever possible the exact amount of ingredients to be used is given, and we know them to be absolutely correct, yet to any user of this book who has failed to obtain satisfactory results or who is in need of still more explicit directions, we will gladly furnish the services of an expert woman, as a correspondent, who will answer all questions, and give any suggestions possible.

In writing, please note carefully the following directions :

1.—Do not forget to give name and Post Office Address.

2.—Address all communications to The Ogilvie Flour Mills Co., Ltd., Baking Dept., Montreal, P.Q.

3.—Name the recipe or recipes for which you wish help, and tell fully the character of the result you obtained.

NOTE.—We cannot be responsible for recipes, if other flour than Ogilvie's Royal Household is used.

To make the Best Bread
you must have the
BEST FLOUR.

When the dough is flat, sour, heavy, will not rise —when the bread is soggy, tasteless, indigestible— then you have cheap and inferior flour.

You may use pure fresh yeast, faithfully adhere to the old-time successful bread making traditions, the methods usually successful—but the baking turns out badly—simply because you have not used the right kind of flour.

Royal Household Flour is thoroughly purified and will yield a sweet, wholesome, light sponge that will bake into light flaky, deliciously flavored, nourishing bread or pastry.

What it is.

Good yeast consists of thousands of tiny plants or germs, and is one of the simplest forms of vegetable life, belonging to the same family as mould and mildew. It is an almost transparent cell, round or oval. filled with sap.

Its Growth.

The growth, which is more frequently spoken of as "fermentation," consists of the reproduction again and again of these little one-celled organisms. This goes on very quickly under proper conditions. One plant buds out from the other sometimes in the form of a chain, or two buds may come from one cell, and in this way the yeast plant multiplies.

Its Care.

While these little yeast cells are tenacious of life they are killed by exposure to extremes of either heat or cold, such as boiling water, or frost, but will keep for many days in a dry, cool place. The best collection of yeast cells massed together in dormant state is the ordinary yeast cake either dry or compressed.

Dried Yeast.

The dried yeast is the best form in which yeast can be obtained for the use of those who live in the country, or in places where it may be necessary to keep the yeast for some length of time. Being dry the cakes cannot decay, but if kept too long the yeast will lose its vitality and die.

Compressed Yeast.

The compressed moist yeast keeps, as a rule, only for a few days. Some of the manufacturers state, however, that it will keep for a month or so if placed under cold water so as to be kept from the air. This form of yeast generally gives the best results, and is more easily used than other forms. In towns it is usually distributed by the manufacturers every two or three days. When fresh it should have a pleasant wine like smell and crisp feeling. If dark and mouldy it is old. If it breaks like putty it is weak.

Its Relation to Bread Making.

For rapid growth it requires a moderately warm moist, sweet, soil such as dough. Sugar hastens the growth, while salt retards it. During its growth it changes some of the starch of the flour into sugar, on which it feeds, at the same time giving off alcohol, and a gas known as Carbon dioxide.

This, in its efforts to escape, expands the elastic gluten (which is a large constituent of flour) and lifts up the dough, or in other words it is "raised."

When the bread is placed in the oven, the heat expands the gas. This is what causes the loaf to "raise" in the oven. Finally the alcohol and gas are driven off, the cell-walls are fixed, and then sweet bread is produced.

BREAD

"With Bread
all griefs are less."

Good bread is the great need of both rich and poor.

It has been man's chief food for thousands of years.

Compared with wheat flour, all other materials are insignificant.

More good nourishment can be purchased for less money than in any other food.

ROYAL HOUSEHOLD excels all others in this respect and should always be used with these recipes.

In the process of bread making, the management and control of the yeast and its fermentation is usually the least understood part of the operation ; and it is owing to mistakes in its treatment that the greater number of failures in bread-making are due.

No manipulation of the flour or dough will compensate for weak or badly prepared yeast.

The other factors of uncertainty in bread-making consist chiefly of insufficient care in kneading and the difference in the quality of flours.

Flour taken from a cold place should be warmed before using to about 75 or 80 degrees.

Have water and milk same temperature. If milk is used it should be scalded and allowed to cool.

Mix thoroughly. Make small loaves and bake well.

HOUSEHOLD WHITE BREAD.

Materials.

8 cups (sifted) Ogilvie's Royal Household,

2 cups water,

2 cups milk,

2 cakes compressed yeast,

3 tablespoons sugar,

1 teaspoon salt,

1 teaspoon butter or lard,

9

Preparation.

Scald the milk and water, and while scalding hot pour the liquid over the butter, sugar and salt. Dissolve the yeast in ¼ cup lukewarm water. When the milk and water have cooled to lukewarm, beat into it four cups of sifted flour with a wooden spoon, add the dissolved yeast and beat well for five minutes. Then stir in flour until the dough is sufficiently stiff to be turned from the mixing bowl to the moulding board in a mass. The quantity of flour to be added may be more or less than the four cups, depending on the temperature and dryness of the flour, Knead the dough thoroughly until it becomes smooth and elastic and ceases to stick to the fingers or moulding board. adding if necessary a little flour from time to time. The kneading should be continued for about fifteen minutes. then put in a well greased earthen bowl, brush lightly with butter, cover with a bread towel and set to rise in a moderately warm place until light or obtains twice its size. This will require about two hours. As soon as bread is light, knead it thoroughly and again place in the earthen bowl and set for another rising until light which will require about one hour. As soon as it is light, form gently into loaves or rolls, place in greased bread pans. brush with melted butter and let stand for one and a half hours, or until very light, then bake in a moderate oven for sixty minutes.

POTATO YEAST No. 1.

Materials for the Yeast.

8 large potatoes.
4 tablespoons Ogilvie's Royal Household.
4 tablespoons salt.
4 tablespoons Granulated sugar.
4 cups (1 quart) boiling water.
16 cups (4 quarts) cold water.
2 cakes of Royal Yeast or 1 cake of compressed.

Preparation.

Peel and boil the potatoes, mash in water boiled in, and, while boiling pour this over the flour, salt and sugar. To this add the boiling water, mix well then add the cold water. Dissolve the yeast in ½ cup lukewarm water and mix with the above. Let this mixture remain in a warm place about eighteen hours, when it is ready for use, keep in a cool place and use as required.

POTATO BREAD No. 1.

Materials for Bread.

>   8 cups (sifted) Ogilvie's Royal Household.
>   1 tablespoon salt.
>   1 tablespoon brown sugar.
>   1 tablespoon butter.
>   4 cups (1 quart) of above liquid.

Preparation.

Set the yeast liquid, on the stove and stir until about blood heat (98 degrees Fahrenheit), then add the salt, sugar, and butter, mix in sufficient of the flour (previously warmed) to make a batter. This will require three to four cups Cover and set to rise. When light and frothy add the balance of the flour or until the dough ceases to stick to the hands or moulding board, kneading thoroughly for about fifteen minutes.

Let rise again until double the original size of dough, when it may be moulded gently into loaves, placed in greased bread pans and brushed with melted butter. Let it stand in a warm place covered with a clean cloth, until it has again doubled its bulk, then bake it in a moderate oven for about sixty minutes.

POTATO YEAST No. 2.

Materials for Yeast.

>   6 large potatoes.
>   ½ cup sugar.
>   2 tablespoons salt.
>   1 cup lukewarm water.
>   1 cake Compressed or two cakes dried yeast.

Preparation.

Peel and grate the potatoes into a porcelain or earthen dish, containing the sugar, and salt. Pour on boiling water until it becomes thick, then let cool until luke-warm. Dissolve the yeast in the lukewarm water and add to the above. Let stand in a warm place for 24 hours when it is ready for use.

POTATO BREAD No. 2.

Materials for Bread.

8 cups (sifted) Ogilvie's Royal Household.
2 cups water.
2 cups milk.
1 tablespoon sugar.
1 tablespoon salt.
1 tablespoon butter or lard.
1 cup of above yeast.

Preparation.

Scald the milk and water, and when cooled to luke-warm add the yeast, salt, sugar and butter and follow the directions given under Potato Bread No. 1.

NOTE.—4 cups of No. 1 or 1 cup of No. 2 Potato Yeast equals 2 cakes Compressed.

GRAHAM BREAD.

Materials.

4 cups graham flour.
3½ cups Ogilvie's Royal Household.
2 tablespoons molasses.
3 cups lukewarm milk.
2 cakes compressed yeast.
1 heaping teaspoon salt.
2 tablespoons brown sugar.
½ teaspoon soda.
2 tablespoons butter.
½ cup lukewarm water.

Preparation.

Sift together the graham flour, wheat flour, brown sugar and salt, then rub in the butter. Add the molasses with the soda dissolved in it. Next add the lukewarm milk, and lastly the yeast dissolved in the lukewarm water.

Knead the dough well for twenty minutes, cover up and set to rise. After rising form it into two loaves, put them in pans and let rise again.

Graham bread requires longer time to rise than white flour bread. Bake in a moderately hot oven for an hour and a quarter.

If graham bread is baked too quickly it is apt to become doughy in the centre.

BOSTON BROWN BREAD

Materials.

 2 cups cornmeal.
 2 cups entire wheat flour.
 1 teaspoon salt.
 1 teaspoon soda.
 1 pint hot water.
 1 cup molasses.
 ½ cake Compressed yeast.
 ½ cup lukewarm water.

Preparation.

Scald the cornmeal with the pint of hot water, then mix in the two cups of entire wheat flour, molasses and salt, adding the yeast, dissolved in ¼ cup lukewarm water. Lastly add the soda, also dissolved in ¼ cup lukewarm water. Pour this batter in greased moulds, filling each a little over half, and let them rise until they are nearly full.

Then put the moulds in a pot of boiling water. Boil three hours, take out and bake them for half an hour.

NOTE.—In boiling let the water come up to the moulds two-thirds of their height, and when it boils away add more boiling water.

SALT RISING BREAD.

Materials for the Yeast.

 2 cups (1 pint) hot water.
 1 teaspoon salt.
 1 heaping tablespoon white cornmeal.
 2½ cups Ogilvie's Royal Household.

Preparation.

Cool the water sufficiently to bear your finger in it, then add the salt, cornmeal, and lastly ten tablespoons of flour. Beat until smooth, then sprinkle the remaining tablespoon of flour over the top of the mixture. Cover and let stand in a warm place five hours. By that time the clear water should have risen on top of the mixture. Drain off this water and beat the mixture thoroughly. Set aside for another hour, at the end of which time the mixture should have become light and frothy. It is now ready for use.

Materials for the Bread.

    10 cups Ogilvie's Royal Household.
    1 heaping tablespoon lard.
    2 cups (1 pint) warm milk.
    ½ teaspoon salt.

Preparation.

    Sift the flour into the mixing bowl, add the salt, and with the tips of your fingers work in the lard. Now make a well in the centre of the flour, pour in your yeast preparation and then the milk. With a spoon begin to stir and continue until it is too stiff to admit of further using the spoon. Turn it out on the moulding board, knead until smooth, divide into four parts and place them in buttered baking pans, having each pan half full. Let rise until they are full. Bake fifty minutes.

CORN BREAD.

Materials.

    2 cups yellow corn-meal.
    2 tablespoons baking powder.
    3 eggs.
    2 tablespoons melted butter.
    2 cups Ogilvie's Royal Household.
    1 teaspoon salt.
    2 cups milk.
    ½ cup boiling water.

Preparation.

    Pour the boiling water over the cornmeal, and let it cool; sift the baking powder, together with the salt and flour. Beat the yolks of the eggs until they are light, and add them to the cornmeal, then add the milk, flour and melted butter, and beat to a smooth batter.

    Beat the whites of the eggs to a stiff froth and add the latter to your mixture, stirring it in quickly. Pour into a shallow well greased pan, and bake in a hot oven over twenty-five minutes.

PARKER HOUSE ROLLS.

Materials.

    3 tablespoons of butter.
    1 tablespoon salt.
    ½ cup lukewarm water.
    6 cups Ogilvie's Royal Household.
    1 pint milk.
    1 tablespoon sugar.
    2 cakes Compressed yeast.

Preparation.

Scald the milk and pour it over the sugar, salt and butter. Allow it to cool, and when it is lukewarm add the yeast, dissolved in the lukewarm water, then add three cups sifted flour. Beat hard, cover and let rise until it is a frothy mass. Then add three cups more flour. Let rise again until it is twice its original bulk, place it on your kneading board. Knead lightly then roll it out one-half an inch thick.

With a biscuit cutter cut out the rolls. Brush each piece with butter, fold and press the edges together, and place them in a greased pan, one inch apart. Let them rise until very light. Bake in a hot oven twenty minutes.

BAKING POWDER BISCUITS.

Materials.

2 cups Ogilvie's Royal Household.
4 teaspoons baking powder.
1 teaspoon salt.
1 cup milk and water (half each).
1 tablespoon butter.
1 tablespoon lard

Preparation.

Sift the flour, salt and baking powder together twice. Cream butter and lard together, and add it to the dry ingredients, using the tips of your fingers. Then add the liquid, mixing with a knife, until you have a very soft dough. Place on your mixing board but do not knead, Roll out lightly until three-fourths of an inch thick. Cut out and bake in a hot oven for fifteen minutes.

CREAM OF TARTAR BISCUITS.

Materials.

4 cups Ogilvie's Royal Household.
2 teaspoons cream of tartar.
1 teaspoon soda.
1 teaspoon salt.
1 tablespoon butter.
1 tablespoon lard.
2 cups ice cold water.

Preparation.

Sift flour, cream of tartar, soda, and salt together
four times so as to thoroughly mix. Work in the butter
and lard with the tips of your fingers. Add the water
(mixing with a knife) until you have a very soft dough.
Turn out on mixing board, do not knead, handling as little
as possible. Roll out three-fourths of an inch thick. Cut
out and bake in a hot oven for twenty minutes.

TEA ROLLS.

Materials.
> 2 cups milk.
> 3 tablespoons butter.
> 2 eggs.
> 1 cake Compressed yeast.
> ½ cup sugar.
> 1 teaspoon salt.
> 6 cups Ogilvie's Royal Household.
> ¼ cup lukewarm water.
> 1 teaspoon ground cinnamon.

Preparation.

Scald the milk and pour it over the sugar, butter and
salt. When it has cooled to lukewarm, beat into it three
cups of flour, sifted three times. Then add the yeast,
dissolved in the lukewarm water. Cover and let rise until
a frothy mass. Add the eggs (well beaten) the balance of
the flour, and the cinnamon.

Place in a buttered bowl. Let rise until twice the
original size. Form into small rolls, place in a buttered
pan, and let rise until very light. Brush the top with
melted butter, bake in a hot oven twenty minutes.

GRIDDLE CAKES.

Material.
> 4 cups sour milk or buttermilk.
> 2 eggs.
> 1 teaspoon salt.
> 2 cups (sifted) Ogilvie's Royal Household.
> 2 tablespoons hot water.

Preparation.

Beat the eggs and salt thoroughly, then add the milk
Stir in the flour, and add the soda dissolved in the hot
water, beat well and cook at once on a very hot griddle.

16

The batter may be dropped on the griddle, with a tablespoon and when brown on one side, quickly turn with a knife.

MUFFINS No. 1.

Materials.

    3 eggs.
    3 tablespoons sugar.
    ¾ cup milk.
    ½ teaspoon salt.
    2 cups Ogilvie's Royal Household.
    2 teaspoons cream tartar.
    1 teaspoon soda.
    1 tablespoon butter.
    2 tablespoons hot water.

Preparation.

    Cream the butter and sugar, and add the beaten yolk of the eggs. Sift the flour, cream tartar, and salt, and mix with the above, at the same time adding the milk, and soda dissolved in the hot water. Lastly add the stiffly beaten whites of eggs, and the butter. Have your gem pans hot and well greased. Bake in a hot oven over twenty minutes.

MUFFINS No. 2.

Materials.

    ⅓ cup butter.
    ¼ cup sugar.
    ¼ teaspoon salt.
    4 tablespoons baking powder.
    1 egg.
    ¾ cup milk.
    2 cups (sifted) Ogilvie's Royal Household.

Preparation.

    Cream the butter and sugar, add the well beaten egg. Sift the flour and baking powder three times, so as to thoroughly mix, and add gradually to the above, together with the milk. Beat thoroughly, turn into hot, greased muffin pans, bake in a hot oven twenty minutes.

    Bad bread can be made from good flour, just as bad flour can be made from good wheat; but good bread cannot be made from bad flour, or good flour from bad wheat.

What Flour Granulation Means in Bread-Making

Flour is composed of myriads of tiny granules.

The small ones absorb yeast, "rise" and "ripen" before the large ones; the result is bread of coarse, poor texture.

ROYAL HOUSEHOLD Flour is perfectly milled, all the flour granules are uniform in size, the sponge rises uniformly, the bread is even in texture, perfect in flavour, good-looking, appetising bread, easily digested.

THE DAILY TEST IN THE LABORATORY AND BAKING DEPARTMENT.
THE OGILVIE FLOUR MILLS COMPANY, LIMITED,
MONTREAL

✎ COOKIES ✎
DOUGHNUTS ETC.

"Of a good beginning cometh
a good end."
JOHN HEYWOOD.—1565.

DOUGHNUTS.

Material.

>2 cups Ogilvie's Royal Household.
>2 eggs.
>1 heaping cup sugar.
>1 cup milk.
>1 teaspoon melted butter.
>2 teaspoons cream of tartar.
>1 teaspoon soda.
>½ nutmeg.

Preparation.

Beat the eggs and sugar together. Dissolve soda in the milk, add the melted butter and mix with above. Sift flour and cream of tartar together twice, beat well and add nutmeg, roll out, cut with doughnut cutter and fry in hot lard.

Care must be taken not to make dough too stiff and it may require slightly more or less flour than the amount given above.

CRUMPETS.

Materials.

>1 cup brown sugar.
>1 cup chopped raisins.
>½ cup butter.
>1 egg.
>½ teaspoon soda.
>2 tablespoons sour milk.
>1½ cup Ogilvie's Royal Household.
>½ (small) teaspoon all kinds spice.

21

Preparation.

Mix sugar, butter, and egg together, then the flour, raisins and spices, add to the above with the soda dissolved in the sour milk. Make rather a stiff dough, drop with a teaspoon on a buttered tin and bake in a hot oven.

MOLASSES COOKIES.

Materials.

1 cup butter.
1 cup sugar.
1 cup molasses.
½ cup milk.
1 egg.
2 teaspoons soda.
4 teaspoons ginger.
4 cups Ogilvie's Royal Household.

Preparation.

Stir together the butter, sugar, egg, and molasses, dissolve soda in the milk and add with the flour, and ginger mixed together. Make moderately stiff dough, roll out not too thin and bake in a moderate oven.

NUT DROP CAKES.

Materials.

1 cup brown sugar.
½ cup butter.
1 cup chopped raisins.
1 cup chopped walnuts.
1¼ cup Ogilvie's Royal Household.
2 eggs.
½ teaspoon soda.
Flavor with cassia, nutmeg, and cloves.

Preparation.

Cream the butter and sugar, and stir in the well beaten eggs, mix the raisins, walnuts, and spices with the flour and add with the soda dissolved in warm water.

Beat thoroughly and drop from a teaspoon on baking pan.

22

CHOCOLATE COOKIES.

Materials.

½ cup butter.
1 tablespoon lard.
1 cup sugar.
¼ teaspoon salt.
1 teaspoon cinnamon.
2 ounces unsweetened chocolate (melted).
1 egg.
½ teaspoon soda.
2 tablespoons milk.
2½ cups Ogilvie's Royal Household.

Preparation.

Beat to a cream the butter and lard, gradually beat into this the sugar, then add the salt, cinnamon and chocolate, now add the well beaten egg, and the soda dissolved in the milk. Stir in enough flour to make a soft dough, cut in round cakes, and bake in rather a quick oven.

The secret of making good cookies is in the use of as little flour as will suffice.

COCOANUT CAKES.

Materials.

1 cocoanut (grated).
Milk of one cocoanut.
Same amount of water.
3¾ cups powdered sugar.
3 eggs (whites).

Preparation.

Dissolve two and one half cups of the sugar in the milk and water, boil until it syrups. Have ready the beaten whites with the balance of sugar, whipped in and add the grated cocoanut little by little beating the boiled syrup all the time. Drop in tablespoonfuls on buttered paper and bake in a slow oven.

CREAM PUFFS.

Material.

½ cup butter.
1 cup water.
1½ cup Ogilvie's Royal Household.
4 eggs.
1 (mustard spoon) soda.
1 teaspoon hot water.

23

Preparation.

Boil water and butter together, and while boiling add flour very slowly, so it will not form in lumps. Stir thoroughly, when cool add the well beaten eggs, and soda dissolved in hot water. Drop on buttered pan size of a walnut, three inches apart. Bake in hot oven over twenty minutes. Don't open the oven until they have been in at least ten minutes, and then as little as possible. If it is too hot put out the fire rather than spoil the cakes by letting the cool air flatten them.

Nothing requires so much care in baking as cream cakes, and nothing gives so much satisfaction as when they are "just right." Never fill them till they are thoroughly cold, then cut open with scissors and fill with mock cream.

MOCK CREAM.

Material.

2 cups milk.
1 cup sugar.
½ cup Ogilvie's Royal Household.
Pinch salt.
2 eggs.
Lemon flavoring.

Preparation.

Put the vessel containing the milk in a pan of hot water on the stove. Mix the flour, salt and sugar together and stir into the milk, stir frequently.

When the water is boiling pour in the egg, beaten very light, stirring briskly while it cooks for a minute or more. If you get it just right it will be light and amy. Flavor with lemon. Dont use until cold.

COOKIES.

Materials.

1 cup sugar
½ cup butter.
4 tablespoons milk.
2 teaspoons baking powder.
2 eggs.
2 cups Ogilvie's Royal Household.
Flavoring.

24

Preparation.

Beat sugar and eggs, together, add the milk, butter, and flavor to taste. Sift baking powder and flour together twice and add gradually to the above until the dough can be handled, when no more flour should be worked in. This may require slightly more or less than the two cups. Roll out thin, cut with a cookie cutter and bake in a quick oven.

HERMITS.

Materials.

½ cup butter.	½ cup currants.
1½ cup sugar.	1 cup raisins (chopped).
3 eggs.	1 small teaspoon cloves.
½ cup milk.	1 small teaspoon cinnamon
2 teaspoons cream tartar.	1 small teaspoon nutmeg
1 teaspoon soda.	3 cups Ogilvie's Royal Household.

Preparation.

Beat eggs and sugar together, add the milk and melted butter, mix other ingredients into the flour and add to the above, making a stiff dough. This may require slightly more or less than the three cups of flour.

Drop on buttered tin in spoonfuls, and bake in a hot oven.

BY ROYAL WARRANT, MILLERS TO H.R.H. THE PRINCE OF WALES.

What is meant by "Protein" in flour?

"Protean in food is the food element that makes bone, muscle and brain.

<u>Pure</u> flour contains more protein, in most useful form, than any other food; but the flour must be pure.

ROYAL HOUSEHOLD Flour is milled to make it the purest in the world: therefore it contains most protein, is most nourishing, is most economical to use.

It pays the housewife to insist upon getting "Royal Household" guaranteed flour, instead of taking a poorer flour which the grocer may be interested in selling.

WHERE ROYAL HOUSEHOLD FLOUR IS MADE.

ROYAL MILLS AND ELEVATOR.   CAPACITY 5000 BARRELS A DAY.
The largest Mill in the British Empire.
MONTREAL.

CAKES

"Dost thou think because thou art
virtuous, there shall be no more cakes?"
—*TWELFTH NIGHT*

Cake-making requires more judgment than any other department of cooking. Nevertheless it is one of the most frequently tried by the beginner.

There are two classes of cakes; those with butter and those without it. The former embraces pound, cup, and fruit cake; to the latter belongs sponge, sunshine, and angel-cake.

Always mix cake in an earthen bowl. The baking of cake requires more care than the mixing. Divide the baking time into quarters; during the first it should begin to rise, the second it should finish rising and begin to brown, in the third it should continue to brown, and during the fourth and last it should finish browning and leave the sides of the pan.

Bake cake with nothing else in the oven and keep it as near the oven centre as possible. Remove the cake from the tin as soon as it leaves the oven, and place it on a sieve or a napkin covered bo rd.

CAKE FILLINGS AND FROSTINGS.

BOILED ICINGS.

Materials.

> 2 cups sugar.
> ¼ cup water.
> Stiffly beaten whites of two eggs.

Preparation.

Boil the sugar and water until it forms a thick syrup, while boiling pour it slowly into the beaten eggs, beating the mixture rapidly all the time. When the mixture has thickened and cooled, it is ready for use in icing cakes.

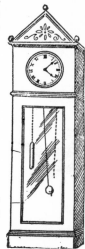

PLAIN FROSTING.

Materials.

 1 egg (white).
 1 teaspoon lemon.
 1 cup pulverized sugar.

Preparation.

 Mix and beat with a fork for five minutes when it is ready for use.

CHOCOLATE FROSTING.

Materials.

 1 cup sugar.
 ½ cup milk.
 ¼ teaspoon cream of tartar.
 2 tablespoons butter.
 1 ounce unsweetened chocolate
 1 teaspoon vanilla.

Preparation.

 Boil the sugar, milk and cream of tartar continuously for six minutes. Remove from stove and stir in the butter, chocolate and vanilla. Beat well, let cool and beat again. The total time of beating should be about one hour.

 This can be put away until required for use, when it may be set in a dish of hot water to soften.

LEMON FILLING No. 1.

Materials.

 1 cup sugar.
 1 egg.
 1 lemon (grated rind and juice).
 ½ cup prepared cocoanut.

Preparation.

 Moisten the cocoanut with milk, and after thoroughly beating the egg place all in a double boiler and cook until the consistency of jelly (about 15 or 20 minutes). The cocoanut flavor makes this a very delicious filling.

LEMON FILLING No. 2.

Materials.

 1 egg yolk.
 1 cup sugar.
 1 lemon (grated rind and juice.)

30

Preparation.

Mix well and place all in a double boiler, cook about twenty minutes, let cool and spread between cakes.

RAISIN FILLING.

Materials.

1 cup raisins.	1 cup sugar.
2 eggs (whites).	Vanilla.

Preparation

Stone and chop raisins, add them to the stiffly beaten eggs, then add enough sugar to make thick. Flavor with Vanilla

ANGEL FOOD.

Materials.

1 cup of egg whites unbeaten.
1½ cups sugar.
Pinch of salt.
1 cup Ogilvie's Royal Household.
1 teaspoon cream tartar.
1 teaspoon flavoring.

Preparation.

Put pinch of salt in egg whites and beat until frothy, put in sugar and cream of tartar, beat again.

Add the flavoring and fold in the flour lightly. Bake in an ungreased pan with a tube, in a moderate oven for thirty-five minutes.

Sift the sugar once, the flour five times, and have the eggs very cold.

SOFT GINGER BREAD.

Materials.

¾ cup molasses.
1 cup brown sugar.
½ cup butter.
1 cup sour milk.
3 eggs.
3 cups Ogilvie's Royal Household.
1 tablespoon ginger.
1 teaspoon cinnamon.
1 teaspoon soda.

Preparation.

Cream the butter and sugar. add the molasses, then the eggs, one at a time, and beat thoroughly.

Put the soda in the sour milk, mixing well, sift the flour and spices, and add to the other mixture, alternating with the milk, beat well. Bake either in Gem pans or in a ginger cake tin.

STRAWBERRY SHORTCAKE.

Materials.

4 teaspoons baking powder.
½ teaspoon salt.
2 tablespoons sugar.
¼ cup butter.
⅛ cup milk.
2 cups Ogilvie's Royal Household.
4 cups strawberries.

Preparation.

Mix flour, baking powder, salt and sugar. and sift twice. Work in butter with fingers. Add milk gradually. Put on board, divide in two parts, and roll out to fit the cake tin, using the least possible flour to roll. Put one part on tin, spread lightly with melted butter, then place other part on top. Bake twenty minutes in hot oven. When baked, the two parts will separate easily without cutting. Mash berries slightly, sweeten and place between cakes, the whole may be covered with whipped cream, and dozen or more whole berries placed on top for a decoration.

WALNUT CAKE.

Materials.

4 eggs (whites).
1½ cups súgar.
½ cup butter.
¾ cup milk.
2 cups Ogilvie's Royal Household.
1 teaspoon cream of tartar.
½ teaspoon soda
1 cup walnuts (chopped).

32

Preparation.

Cream the butter and sugar thoroughly, add the stiffly beaten whites of eggs, then the milk. Sift the flour, cream of tartar, and soda together twice, and add to the above, mixing well, lastly add the chopped walnuts. Bake in a moderate oven forty minutes or more.

SPONGE CAKE.

Materials.

6 eggs.
3 cups sugar.
4 cups Ogilvie's Royal Household.
1 cup cold water.
2 teaspoons cream of tartar.
1 teaspoon soda.
Flavoring.

Preparation.

Beat eggs until very light, add sugar and beat again, sift the flour and cream of tartar together three times. Dissolve soda in the water, and add to the eggs and sugar mixing in the flour at once, flavor to taste and bake in a moderate oven for thirty minutes or more.

LOAF CAKE.

Materials.

4 eggs.
5 cups Ogilvie's Royal Household.
2 cups sugar.
1 cup molasses.
1½ cups butter.
1 cup new milk.
1 lb. raisins stoned and chopped.
¼ lb. citron, chopped.
Spice as desired.
1 teaspoon soda.

Preparation.

Cream butter and sugar. Mix in the molasses and spices together with the eggs well beaten.

Dissolve soda in milk and add to the above. Dredge raisins and the citron in one cup of flour, and thoroughly mix in together with balance of flour. Bake in a slow oven for one hour.

FIG CAKE.

Materials.
>1 cup butter.
>2 cups sugar.
>3 cups Ogilvie's Royal Household.
>4 eggs (whites).
>1 cup milk.
>2 teaspoons baking powder.

Preparation.
Cream butter and sugar, add flour with baking powder sifted twice, alternating it with the milk, beat well and lastly add whites of eggs beaten stiff.
Bake in two tins.

FILLING FOR ABOVE.

Material.
>¾ lb. figs.
>¾ cup sugar.
>½ cup boiling water.

Preparation.
Chop figs fine, add sugar and boiling water, cook on stove until a smooth paste, if too stiff add more water. when cold spread between cakes.

PLAIN POUND CAKE.

Materials.
>1 lb. (2 cups) granulated sugar.
>1 lb. (2 cups) softened butter.
>1 lb. (4 cups) Ogilvie's Royal Household.
>9 eggs.
>Lemon flavoring.

Preparation.

Beat the eggs thoroughly, add sugar and beat again, then the butter, lastly the flour, flavor to taste.
Beat thoroughly as each ingredient is added as upon this depends the quality of the cake.
Bake for thirty minutes or more in a moderate oven.

ONE EGG CAKE.

Materials.

½ cup milk.
1 cup sugar.
1 cup Ogilvie's Royal Household.
2 teaspoons baking powder.
2 tablespoons melted butter.
Flavoring.

Preparation.

Beat the egg until light, and add to the sugar, stir until dissolved, then add milk. Sift flour and baking powder twice, mix well with above, and lastly add the melted butter, flavor to taste, bake in a flat pan.

CHOCOLATE CAKE.

Materials

1½ cup sugar.
½ cup butter.
3 eggs.
¾ cup milk.
2 cups Ogilvie's Royal Household.
1 teaspoon cream of tartar.
½ teaspoon soda.
1 ounce unsweetened chocolate.

Preparation.

Cream the butter and sugar, and add the well beaten eggs, (saving out the white of one) then the milk. Sift the flour, cream of tartar and soda together twice, and mix thoroughly with the above, warm the chocolate over tea-kettle and stir into the batter, bake about thirty-five minutes, in a moderate oven.

Let cool and split in two with a sharp knife, frost each part with the following:—

FILLING FOR CHOCOLATE CAKE.

Material.

1 cup sugar.
4 tablespoons water.
1 egg (white).
2 ounces of unsweetened chocolate.
Pinch cream tartar.

Preparation.

Mix sugar, cream tartar and water, boil until it threads, beat the white of an egg very stiff, stir syrup in slowly and beat until thick, then spread on cake, make another frosting like first, add the two squares of chocolate to it. Cover the white frosting with the chocolate frosting, and lift one part of cake on the other, press together.

DAYTON CAKE.

Materials.

1 cup butter.

2 cups sugar.

3½ cups Ogilvie's Royal Household.

¾ cup milk.

1½ cups raisins.

1 cup walnuts, meats.

5 eggs.

2 teaspoons cream of tartar.

1 teaspoon soda.

1 nutmeg

Preparation.

Beat the eggs well, and add to the butter, and sugar previously creamed. Sift flour, cream of tartar and soda together twice and add, alternating with the milk.

Chop walnuts and raisins together and mix in lastly, then add grated nutmeg.

JELLY ROLL.

Materials.

¾ cup sugar.

3 eggs.

1 cup Ogilvie's Royal Household.

1 teaspoon cream of tartar.

½ teaspoon soda.

1 tablespoon hot water.

Pinch of salt.

Preparation.

Beat the eggs until light, add the sugar and salt and stir until dissolved. Sift the flour and cream of tartar together twice, add to the above and beat until light, then add the soda, dissolved in hot water, put in a flat pan, bake ten or fifteen minutes.

Take out on a napkin, spread the under side with jelly and roll up.

SNOW-BALL CAKE.

Materials.

½ cup butter.
1 cup sugar.
½ cup milk.
2 cups Ogilvie's Royal Household.
1 teaspoon cream of tartar.
½ teaspoon soda.
4 eggs (whites).

Preparation.

Cream the butter and sugar thoroughly, add the stiffly beaten whites of the eggs, then the milk. Sift the flour, cream of tartar and soda together three times, add to the above, mixing thoroughly. Bake in a moderate oven thirty minutes or more.

FRUIT CAKE.

Materials.

2 cups (one pound) butter.
2½ cups (one pound) brown sugar.
4 cups (one pound) Ogilvie's Royal Household.
10 eggs.
2½ pounds raisins.
2½ pounds currants.
¾ pound citron.
1 ounce mace.
½ ounce nutmeg.
2 teaspoons cloves.
1 teaspoon cinnamon.
1 teaspoon allspice.
1 cup molasses.
1 teaspoon soda.

Preparation.

Cream the butter and sugar, add the well beaten eggs then the molasses, with the soda dissolved in it. Mix flour with balance of materials and add to the above, mix thoroughly and bake in a very slow oven for six hours.

CHEAP FRUIT CAKE.

Materials.

1 cup sugar.
1 cup sour milk.
½ cup butter.
1 cup raisins.
1 teaspoon soda.
½ teaspoon salt.
½ teaspoon all kinds of spice.
2 cups Ogilvie's Royal Household.

Preparation.

Cream the butter and sugar, add the sour milk, with soda and salt dissolved in it, then the flour mixed with spices, currants and raisins. Mix thoroughly and bake.

Whether the yeast is all right or all wrong, means whether the bread will be good or bad. Look out for these little things if you want your baking to be always successful.

GRINDING FLOOR, ROYAL MILLS.
THE OGILVIE FLOUR MILLS COMPANY, LIMITED,
MONTREAL.

PASTRY & PIES

The digestibility of pies has been called into question, but when properly made pies are as easily digested as anything else.

Until quite recently it has been taken for granted, by the majority of people, that it was impossible to make good pastry out of Manitoba wheat flour without using a large amount of shortening.

They have thought it necessary to keep two kinds of flour, one for bread, and the other for pastry. This idea is erroneous.

ROYAL HOUSEHOLD makes the most delicious pastry when same amount of shortening is used as with ordinary pastry flour. Try it with the following recipes.

Paste for pies should be kept cold, rolled quite thin and a little larger than the tin to allow for shrinkage. Allow more paste for the upper than the under crust, and be sure to perforate the former. Always brush around the edge of the undercrust with cold water and press the upper one down on it. When baking a juicy fruit pie make an incision in the centre and place a small funnel-shaped piece of paper into it.

This will keep the juice from escaping at the sides of the pie. Never grease a pie tin. Properly made pastry will grease its own tin.

PLAIN PIE CRUST.

Materials.

2 cups (sifted) Royal Household.
½ cup ice cold water.
6 level tablespoons butter.
6 level tablespoons lard.
½ teaspoon salt.

Preparation.

Mix salt with flour, with two knives cut in shortening, leaving it rather large; with knife stir in water little at a time; do it quickly.

PUFF PASTE.

Materials.

4 cups (1 pound) Ogilvie's Royal Household.
2 cups (1 pound) butter.
1 cup ice cold water.

Preparation.

Wash the butter thoroughly or until free from salt. Put both flour and butter in a cold place. Keep all utensils ice cold while working the dough. This is important. Mix about one-fourth of the butter into the flour, adding enough ice cold water to make a nice paste. Roll out thin and spread more butter on with a knife; fold up as you would a piece of paper, repeating this until all the butter is worked in.

It is well to roll thoroughly, as better results will be obtained, half an hour is none too long. The dough then should be put in a cold place for several hours, over night is better, but do not allow it to freeze.

Bake in a moderately hot oven.

LEMON PIE.

Materials.

6 tablespoons water.
6 tablespoons sugar.
1½ tablespoons cornstarch.
1 teaspoon butter.
1½ tablespoons lemon juice (half lemon).

Preparation.

Beat yolk of egg until light yellow, then add water Mix sugar and cornstarch in saucepan, add yolk, water and butter. Cook until a clear paste, then add lemon when nearly done. Use pastry receipt for pie crust.

LEMON CREAM PIE.

Materials.

4 eggs.
1 cup sugar.
2 heaping tablespoons flour.
1½ cup boiling water.
The grated rind and juice of two lemons.

Preparation.

Beat the yolks and whites of the eggs, separately. To the beaten yolks add the sugar, flour, lemon juice, rind, and lastly the boiling water. Cook in a double boiler and when it begins to thicken, add to it one-half of the beaten whites. Stir this in thoroughly and let it cook until it is as thick as desired.

Use the remainder of the whites for the Meringue on top of the pie. After the custard has cooled, fill a baked shell, pile the meringue on top, and bake in a very slow oven until the meringue is brown.

MERINGUE.

Material.

2 eggs (white).
4 tablespoons icing sugar.

Preparation.

Beat stiff but not dry, adding sugar all the time. Put on top of filling and brown slightly in oven. It is important to have everything cold.

APPLE PIE.

Materials.

4 large apples.
1 cup sugar.
½ nutmeg (grated).
1 teaspoon butter.
Pie paste.

Preparation.

Line a deep pie tin with nice paste, (recipe found elsewhere), select large tart apples, pare and slice, put an even layer of these slices in the prepared tin, sprinkle with sugar, dot with butter, dust with nutmeg, cover with paste, press closely around edges, bake in a moderate oven for forty-five minutes.

PUMPKIN PIE.

Materials.

3 eggs.
1 cup sugar.
1 cup stewed pumpkin (strained).
1 teaspoon ginger.
1 teaspoon cinnamon.
½ teaspoon cloves.
2 cups milk.

Preparation.

Beat the eggs, add to them the sugar, pumpkin, and spices. Beat thoroughly, then add the milk, mix well, bake in a raw crust, in a moderately hot oven for thirty minutes or more. This will make two small or one large pie.

MINCE PIE.

Materials.

4 lbs. beef tenderloin.	15 large apples, chopped fine.
2 lbs. suet.	
3 lbs. brown sugar.	2 lbs. citron, sliced.
3 lbs. seeded raisins.	Grated rind and juice of four lemons.
3 lbs. currants.	
1 oz. mace	Grated rind and juice of 4 oranges
1 oz. nutmeg.	1 quart brandy.
1 oz. cinnamon.	1 pint Maderia wine.
1 oz. cloves.	1 tablespoon salt.

Preparation.

Boil the beef until well done, when cold, chop it fine. Chop suet and apples and add to the beef. Mix the sugar and spices and add to them the wine, brandy, lemon and orange juice.

Mix the raisins, currants, citron, lemon and orange rinds.

Now combine gradually the three sets of ingredients after having added the salt to the liquid part, using a small portion of each until all are used.

Pack in stone jars, cover closely and keep in a dry cool closet. This will keep a long time.

WINNIPEG MILLS.   CAPACITY 3,500 BARRELS FLOUR PER DAY.
THE OGILVIE FLOUR MILLS COMPANY, LIMITED.
WINNIPEG, MANITOBA.

PUDDINGS

*"The proof of the pudding
is the eating."*

PAN-DOWDY.

Materials.

Pie paste.
Tart apples, peeled and sliced.
2 teaspoons butter.
1 cup of molasses (more or less to taste).
Nutmeg or any preferred spice.

Preparation.

Line a pan about ten inches square, and four deep with the paste. Fill with the apples, and distribute the butter in small pieces over the top, spice to taste, and pour the molasses over the apples. Cover with puff paste, and bake slowly for two hours. To be eaten hot with cream.

NOTE.—Recipes for paste given elsewhere.

QUEEN OF PUDDINGS.

Materials.

4 cups bread crumbs.
4 cups milk.
4 eggs (yolks).
1 teaspoon butter.
1 lemon (grated rind only).
1 cup sugar.

Preparation.

Soak bread crumbs in milk until soft. Beat the eggs, sugar and salt together, add to the bread and milk with the butter and lemon. Mix thoroughly, and bake in a quick oven but do not let it get watery. After it is cooked spread with jelly, frost with the following if desired.

47

FROSTING.

Materials.
>4 eggs (whites).
>1 lemon (juice).
>½ cup sugar.

Preparation.
>Mix all together and whip until light.

ORANGE BAVARIAN CREAM.

Materials.
>½ box gelatine.
>½ cup cold water.
>4 sour oranges.
>Boiling water.
>Sugar.
>Cracked ice.
>2 cups cream.

Preparation.
>Soak the gelatine in cold water for half an hour. Take the juice of the oranges, and add half the grated peel of one, add sufficient boiling water to make two cups, sweeten to taste and while hot add the gelatine. When thoroughly dissolved set in a pan of cracked ice to cool, stirring from time to time. Whip the cream until very stiff, and when jelly begins to thicken add it by degrees to the cream, stirring briskly until well mixed, then mould.

RUSSIAN CREAM.

Materials.
>⅓ box gelatine.
>2 cups milk.
>1 teaspoon vanilla.
>4 eggs.
>½ cup sugar.
>Hot water.

Preparation.
>Dissolve the gelatine in hot water. Beat yolk of the eggs separate with the sugar, stir in the milk and make into a custard, using a double boiler.

Before removing from the stove mix in the dissolved gelatine and vanilla. Beat whites of the eggs to a stiff froth, strain the custard into them then stir all together. Pour into small moulds, set away to cool. Serve very cold.

PLUM PUDDING.

Materials.

½ lb. bread crumbs.
½ lb. suet, chopped.
½ lb. sugar.
4 eggs.
½ lb. seeded raisins.
½ lb. currants.
½ lb. figs, chopped.
1 cup milk.

¼ lb. citron, sliced.
½ cup brandy.
1 teaspoon nutmeg.
½ teaspoon cinnamon.
½ teaspoon cloves.
¼ teaspoon mace.
1 teaspoon salt.

Preparation.

Scald the milk and pour it over the crumbs, cream the suet, add the sugar and the well beaten yolks of the eggs. When milk and crumbs are cool, combine them with the other mixture, then add the raisins, figs, currants, citron, salt and spices.

Add the brandy, and lastly, the stiffly-beaten whites of the eggs. Pour into a buttered mould and steam five hours, serve with hard sauce.

HARD SAUCE.

Materials.

½ cup butter.
1 cup sugar (powdered).
1 teaspoon vanilla.

Preparation.

Cream sugar and butter together, add vanilla. Set on ice until wanted.

SUET PUDDING.

Materials.

1 cup suet.
1 cup sour milk.
2 eggs.
1 teaspoon soda.
½ teaspoon salt.
½ teaspoon grated nutmeg.

1 cup molasses.
3 cups Ogilvie's Royal Household.
½ cup sugar.
1 cup raisins (chopped)
1 teaspoon ginger.
½ teaspoon cloves.

Preparation.

Beat the eggs, add the sugar, then the suet, chopped very fine, then the molasses, and after it the flour. Dissolve the soda in the sour milk and add it to the mixture, lastly add the spices and raisins.

Pour into a buttered mould and steam three hours. Serve with the following sauce.:

FOAMY SAUCE.

Materials.
>   1 egg.
>   1 cup sugar (powdered).
>   ¼ cup milk (hot).
>   Vanilla flavoring.

Materials.

Beat the egg, and add sugar slowly. Just before serving add hot milk and flavoring.

TRILBY PUDDING.

Materials.
>   2 cups cream.
>   1 pound walnuts.
>   1 pound marshmallows.
>   ½ cup sugar (powdered).
>   Vanilla.

Preparation.

Whip the cream very stiff. Cut marshmallows as fine as possible with scissors, dip frequently in sugar to keep from sticking, mix all together and mould. Decorate with canned cherries.

MACAROON PUDDING.

Materials.

½ lb. macaroons.	Sherry wine.
2 eggs.	5 tablespoons sugar.
¼ teaspoon salt.	1 cup milk.
1 cup cream.	2 tablespoons almonds
¼ teaspoon almond ex-	blanched & chopped.
tract.	

Preparation.

Soak a dozen macaroons ten minutes in cherry wine, and then remove them. Beat two eggs slightly, add the sugar, salt, milk and cream, then the chopped almonds, the almond extract and four finely-powdered macaroons. Turn this mixture into a pudding dish, arrange soaked macaroons on top, cover and bake thirty minutes in a hot oven.

BAKED APPLE DUMPLINGS.

Material.

4 cups Ogilvie's Royal Household.
¾ cup butter.
1½ cup milk.
1 tablespoon Baking powder.
Apples.
Nutmeg.

Preparation.

Pare, quarter and core the apples. Sift flour, and baking powder together twice, mix in the butter and add sufficient milk to make quite a stiff paste (This may require slightly more or less than one and one-half cups.) Roll out about one-fourth inch thick, cut in large round pieces. Put several pieces of apple in each and fold into a ball, and bake in the following syrup.:

SYRUP.

Material.

4 cups water.
1 cup sugar.
1 teaspoon butter (heaping)

Preparation.

Put all together in a baking tin, set on the stove and let come to a boil, then drop in the dumplings and bake in a hot oven. Serve warm with sugar and cream.

PUDDING SAUCE.

Materials.

1 cup sugar.
4 teaspoons corn starch.
1 lemon.
1 tablespoon butter.
4 tablespoons water.

Preparation.

Boil the sugar, moistened with the water, **five** minutes. Add the corn starch, dissolved in a little cold water, cook eight or ten minutes. Add lemon juice, grated rind and the butter, stir until the butter is melted. Serve at once.

GLENORA MILLS,   CAPACITY 2,000 BARRELS FLOUR PER DAY.
THE OGILVIE FLOUR MILLS COMPANY, LIMITED,
MONTREAL.

SOUPS

"Too many cooks
spoil the broth."

Soups are of two classes. Soups made with "stock" and soups without.

To the former class belong bouillon, brown stock, white stock, consomme and lambstock or mutton-broth.

Soups without stocks are classed as cream soups, purees, and bisques.

WHITE STOCK.

Materials.

4 lbs. knuckle of veal.	1 small onion.
1 lb. lean beef.	2 stalks celery.
10 cups cold water.	1 bayleaf.
10 pepper corns.	1 tablespoon salt.

Preparation.

Remove the meat from the bone and cut in small pieces. Put meat and bone into a kettle, add the water, and prepared vegetables. Bring it slowly to a boil and skim carefully. Simmer for five hours. Strain twice through several thicknesses of cheesecloth and the stock will be clear. White stock can also be made from the water in which a fowl or chicken is cooked.

CREAM OF TOMATO SOUP.

Materials.

2 cups milk.
1½ tablespoons butter.
1 tablespoon flour..
1 cup tomatoes.
½ salt spoon soda.
½ teaspoon sugar.
½ teaspoon salt and pepper.

Preparation.

Put milk in double boiler, mix the flour and butter together, add to the milk when boiling.

Cook tomatoes twenty minutes, then strain, now add soda, sugar, salt and pepper. Add to the milk and serve immediately.

SPLIT PEA SOUP.

Materials.

1 cup dried split peas.
8 cups cold water.
2 cups milk.
1 small onion.
2 tablespoons butter.

1 teaspoon salt.
¼ teaspoon white pepper.
2-inch cube salt pork.
2 tablespoons flour.

Preparation.

Soak the peas over night, drain and add water, pork and onion sliced. Simmer until the peas are very soft, then rub through a sieve. Cream butter and flour together and add to the peas. Then add salt, pepper and milk. Reheat and serve hot.

POTATO SOUP.

Materials.

3 potatoes.
4 cups milk.
1 onion.
2 stalks celery.

1 teaspoon salt.
¼ teaspoon pepper
2 tablespoons butter.
1 tablespoon flour.

Preparation.

Cook the potatoes in salted water with the onion. When soft mash smooth and rub through a fine sieve. Scald the milk with the celery. Remove the celery, add the butter and flour creamed together. Then add the prepared potatoes to the milk and season with salt and pepper. Let come to a boil and serve at once.

BROWN STOCK.

Materials.

5 lbs. shin beef.	⅛ cup potato.
8 cups (½ gallon water).	⅛ cup turnip.
10 pepper corns.	⅛ cup onion.
5 cloves.	⅛ cup carrot.
1 bay leaf.	⅛ cup celery.
1 tablespoon salt.	coarsely chopped.
2 sprigs parsley.	

Preparation.

Cut the lean meat into small pieces and brown it in a hot frying pan, using the marrow from the bone. Put the bone and fat in the kettle. Add the cold water and let it stand twenty minutes.

Put over the fire and bring to the boiling point, remove the scum as it rises and add the browned meat. Cover the kettle. Reduce heat and cook at the boiling point for five hours. Add the prepared vegetables and seasoning and cook for two hours. Strain immediately.

OXTAIL SOUP.

Materials.

1 oxtail cut in small pieces.	1 teaspoon salt.
	¼ teaspoon pepper.
5 cups brown stock.	½ cup Maderia wine.
Carrot cut in dice.	1 teaspoon Worcestershire sauce.
Celery cut in dice.	
Onion cut in dice.	Juice of half lemon.
Turnip cut in dice.	Butter.

Preparation.

Dredge the oxtail in flour and fry in butter until nicely browned. Add it to the stock and simmer two hours. Parboil the vegetables ten minutes, drain and add them to the stock. Cook until the vegetables are tender, then add salt, pepper, wine, sauce and lemon juice. Let it cook ten minutes and serve.

ORANGE SOUP.

Materials.

2 cups orange juice.
2 cups water
4 tablespoons sugar.
1 tablespoon arrowroot.

Preparation.

Bring the orange juice and water to the boiling point. Add the arrowroot wet with a little cold water. Cook one minute and strain, add the sugar and put away to cool, when ready to serve put a table spoon of cracked ice in a lemonade glass and pour in the orange soup.

Currant, raspberry and blackberry soups may be made the same way. Excellent for summer luncheon.

OYSTER COCKTAILS.

Materials.

½ doz. small oysters with liquor.
1 teaspoon lemon juice.
3 drops Tabasco Sauce.
1 teaspoon Worcestershire Sauce.
1 dessert spoon Tomato Sauce.

Preparation.

Strain liquor, put all together in a glass, stir well and serve very cold.

BOUILLON.

Materials.

3 lbs. lean beef.
2 lbs. lean veal.
1 lb. marrowbone.
6 cups cold water.
10 pepper corns.
1 tablespoon salt.

⅓ cup potatoes.
⅓ cup celery.
⅓ cup onion.
⅓ cup turnip
finely chopped.

Preparation.

Put the meat, marrowbone and water into the soup kettle and let it stand covered for one hour. Heat slowly to the boiling point. Remove the scum and cook for four hours. Add the vegetables and seasoning and cook two hours. Strain and allow it to get cold, then remove the fat. Serve in cups.

GREEN PEA SOUP.

Materials.

2 cans peas.	2 cups hot milk.
1 onion.	1 cup cream.
1 saltspoon pepper.	1 bay leaf.
1 tablespoon salt.	1 sprig parsley.
1 teaspoon sugar.	2 cups chicken stock.
3 tablespoons butter.	Small amount mace.

3 tablespoons Ogilvie's Royal Household.

Preparation.

Set aside one cup of peas and put remainder in a stew-pan with the onion, pepper, salt, sugar and seasoning. Let simmer for one-half hour, remove herbs, mash the peas and add the stock. Let it come to a boil, then add the butter and flour cooked together, let simmer ten minutes and strain through a sieve. Return to stove, add the cup of whole peas, the hot milk and cream, serve at once.

BY ROYAL WARRANT, MILLERS TO H.R.H. THE PRINCE OF WALES.

The right way is the easy way

There is always a right way—and several wrong ways—of doing most everything. This is true of pastry.

The right way—and the easy way—of making faultless pastry, is the "Royal Household" way. You probably know some of the wrong ways from experience.

"ROYAL HOUSEHOLD" Flour makes ideal pastry—the lightest, most inviting, most delicious Cakes, Pies, Doughnuts, etc.—you ever ate. And it is just as simple as A B C.

Follow the recipes in this cook book—add enough ice-cold water to keep the dough from being tough and springy—work the dough thoroughly, and you will have better pastry than any so-called "pastry flour" will make.

FORT WILLIAM MILL, UNDER CONSTRUCTION.   CAPACITY 4,000 BARRELS PER DAY.
THE OGILVIE FLOUR MILLS COMPANY, LIMITED,
FORT WILLIAM, ONT.

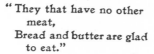

MEATS AND FOWLS

" They that have no other
meat,
Bread and butter are glad
to eat."

Next to bread, meat forms the principal food on our tables.

Always remember that the cheaper parts of a first class animal may be prepared to furnish far better dishes than the high priced portions of an inferior animal; in other words, a stew from the forequarter of a first-class animal will be better than a roast from the loin of an inferior animal, and it will be cheaper.

If meat is tough, soak in vinegar and water for six or seven hours in proportion of one and one half-pints of vinegar to six quarts of water.

Always cut across the grain of the muscle.

Never wash fresh meat before roasting. Scrape if necessary to clean it. If it has been wet, wipe thoroughly dry before cooking.

Do not put meat directly on ice, place in a vessel.

BEEFSTEAK PIE.

Materials.

> 2 lbs. round steak ½ inch thick.
> 1 onion sliced.
> 1 heaping tablespoon flour.
> 2 tablespoons butter.
> 2 medium potatoes sliced thin.
> 1 teaspoon salt.
> ½ teaspoon pepper.

Preparation.

Cut the steak into strips one and one-half inch long and one inch wide, place in a saucepan, cover with boiling water add the sliced onion and simmer until

63

the meat is tender. Remove the meat, discard onion, add potatoes to the liquid and parboil six minutes then remove the potatoes. Measure the liquor and add enough boiling water, to make one pint, add the seasonings. Cream the butter and flour together, add to the liquor and cook five minutes. In the bottom of a pudding dish, place a layer of one-half the potatoes, and on top of this arrange the meat, placing the other half of the potatoes on top of it. Pour over this sufficient gravy to entirely cover the contents of the baking dish. When cool cover with a crust and bake in a hot oven.

The crust is made as follows:

Materials.
   1 cup Ogilvie's Royal Household.
   1 rounding tablespoon butter.
   1 rounding tablespoon lard.
   ½ teaspoon salt.
   1 teaspoon baking powder.
   Milk.

Preparation.
  Sift flour, baking powder and salt. Cream butter and lard together and combine them with the dry ingredients, mixing thoroughly with finger tips. Add enough milk to make a soft dough, roll out about one-quarter of an inch thick, and cover with it the contents of the pudding dish.

BEEF LOAF.

Materials.
   3 lbs. lean beef.
   ½ lb. raw ham.
   3 eggs well beaten.
   3 soda crackers rolled fine.
   1 teaspoon salt.
   1 teaspoon pepper.
   3 tablespoons cream.
   6 hard boiled eggs.

Preparation.
  Chop the beef and ham very fine, add salt and pepper, cracker crumbs, the well beaten eggs and cream. Mix all together thoroughly. Grease a bread

pan, and press half the mixture into it firmly. Trim each end of the hard boiled eggs so as to make a flat surface, then put on top of the mixture in the bread pan, placing them in a row, end to end. Now pack on to the balance of the meat, pressing it down well. Cover and bake in a moderate oven over one hour. Uncover and bake half an hour longer.

Serve either hot or cold.

HAMBURG STEAK.

Materials.

2 lbs. round steak.
1 teaspoon salt.
½ teaspoon pepper.
½ cup boiling water.
1 teaspoon onion juice.
1 egg.
½ cup Ogilvie's Royal Household.
½ cup drippings.

Preparation.

Chop the meat very fine, add the seasonings. Beat the egg and mix it with the meat. Divide into four equal portions and shape in round cakes, about one inch thick. Dredge these on both sides with flour and fry in the drippings, turning them as to brown both sides. When nicely browned add the half cup of boiling water. Cover closely and simmer for forty-five minutes.

POT ROAST BEEF.

Materials.

5 lbs. beef.
½ lb. suet.
6 cloves.
2 bay leaves.
2 slices onion.
1 carrot chopped fine.
1 tablespoon flour.
1 pint boiling water.
Salt and pepper.

65

Preparation.

Put the suet in a kettle, add the onion, bay-leaves, cloves and chopped carrot; let it cook five minutes and get very hot. Put in the meat well seasoned with salt and pepper and brown it on both sides. Add the water, cover closely and simmer until very tender. Remove from the pot and thicken the liquor with the flour. Strain and serve it in a sauceboat.

NOTE.—As the roast cooks add boiling water to keep the quantity the same as the first.

VEAL LOAF.

Materials.

3 lbs. lean veal.
¼ lb. salt pork.
2 eggs well beaten.
3 soda crackers rolled fine.
1 teaspoon salt.
1 teaspoon pepper.
3 tablespoons cream.
2 tablespoons boiling water.

Preparation.

Chop the veal and pork very fine, then add the salt, pepper, cracker crumbs, well beaten eggs, cream, and hot water. Mix all together very thoroughly, grease an earthenware pan and pack the mixture into it, pressing it down firmly. Cover and bake in a moderate oven one hour. Uncover and bake half an hour longer. Serve either hot or cold in slices.

CORN BEEF HASH.

Materials.

1 pint chopped cold corned beef.
½ teaspoon salt.
¼ cup cream.
1 pint cold chopped potatoes.
½ teaspoon pepper.
1 tablespoon butter.
Onion.

Preparation.

Rub inside of the frying pan with a cut onion. Put in the butter and let it get hot, add the meat, potatoes, salt and pepper, having them well mixed.

Moisten the whole with the cream, spread evenly and place the pan so that the hash can brown slowly and evenly underneath. When done, fold over and turn out on the platter.

The browning can be done in the oven if preferred.

BOILED BEEFSTEAK.

Materials.

1 porterhouse steak.
2 tablespoons butter.
1 teaspoon salt.
1 teaspoon pepper.

Preparation.

Before broiling beat the steak with a rolling pin sufficient to soften the fibre. Have the pan very hot at first, turn constantly to prevent burning, broil from seven to ten minutes. Place on a very hot platter, put the butter in pieces over the top, press it in with the point of a knife, sprinkle over the pepper and salt, serve in its own gravy.

CHICKEN PIE.

Materials.

1 chicken, about 4 pounds.
2 tablespoons butter.
Pepper and salt.
Flour.

Preparation.

Remove all fat from chicken, cut up and put into boiling water. Add pepper and salt as desired. Cook until the meat can be removed from the bones easily. Skim out of the water, cool, and pick into small pieces and remove all bones. There should be about one quart of liquid left in the kettle for gravy. To this add flour enough to make a thick gravy. Add the two tablespoons of butter or more, more if wanted rich, pour over the chicken and let cool.

PASTE FOR CHICKEN PIE.

Materials.

3 cups Ogilvie's Royal Household.
2 teaspoons cream tartar.
1 teaspoon soda.
1 teaspoon salt (heaping.)
¼ cup butter.
¼ cup lard.
Sweet milk.

Preparation.

Sift together the flour, cream tartar, soda, and salt. Rub the butter and lard in very fine, then add sufficient sweet milk to make a moderately soft dough. Line a deep baking dish, fill with the cold mixture and cover. Bake an hour or more. Do not forget to make several air holes in the top of crust, if air tight gases collect that makes the pie poisonous.

Veal pie can be made in the same way.

CREAM CHICKEN.

Materials.

1 chicken (ordinary size).
1 can mushrooms.
2 cups cream.
1 cup milk.
4 tablespoons Ogilvie's Royal Household.
2 tablespoons butter.
1 onion (grated).
Nutmeg, black and red pepper.

Preparation.

Boil chicken, and when cold cut as for salad. Put cream and milk in a saucepan, let come to a boil. In another pan put the butter and when melted add the flour. Pour the boiling milk and cream over the butter and flour, flavor with the onion and a little grated nutmeg. Season very highly with black and red pepper, Mix chicken, mushrooms and sauce together and put in a baking dish, cover with grated bread crumbs and small pieces of butter, bake about twenty minutes or until brown.

ROAST GOOSE.

Materials.

1 large goose.	Pepper.
6 strips salt pork.	Stuffing.
1 cup water.	Apple sauce.
Salt.	Watercress.

Preparation.

Scrub the goose with hot soap suds, then draw, wash thoroughly in cold water and wipe dry. Stuff, truss, sprinkle with salt and pepper and cover the entire breast with the strips of salt pork. Place on the rack in dripping pan, pour the water into the latter under the goose. Bake in a hot oven for two hours and a half, basting every ten minutes. Remove the pork the last half hour. Garnish the dish with watercress and serve with apple sauce.

The receipe for stuffing made of potatoes is given herein.

POTATO STUFFING
For Fowl.

Materials.

2 cups hot mashed potatoes.	¼ cup butter.
	1 teaspoon salt.
1 cup crumbs.	½ teaspoon sage.
¼ cup salt pork, chopped.	1 egg.
1 teaspoon onion juice.	

Preparation.

Add to the potatoes the butter, egg, salt, onion juice, sage, crumbs and pork, mix thoroughly and use as stuffing.

FRIED SPRING CHICKEN.

Materials.

1 chicken.
½ cup flour.
1 cup lard.
Pepper and salt.

Preparation.

Select a large plump spring chicken. Draw and cut into the natural joints. Put into ice water for five minutes. Drain and place on a platter in the ice box for two hours. Dredge thickly with flour, and sprinkle with salt and pepper. Place the lard in a frying pan and when it is hot saute the chicken in it, taking care to turn it often. so it will not brown, cook thoroughly, serve with cream gravy.

Some prefer frying bacon enough with the chicken to make the required amount of fat. If you do so, serve some of the bacon with the chicken.

OYSTER STUFFING.

Materials.

10 crackers.
½ cup butter.
1 cup oysters.
Salt and seasoning.

Preparation.

Roll the crackers fine, turn over sufficient boiling water until every part is moistened. Add the butter, salt, and season to taste, lastly add the oysters chopped.

Mix thoroughly.

DRESSING FOR TURKEY.

Materials.

6 cups bread crumbs.
¼ lb. salt pork.
2 tablespoons butter.
3 eggs.
Salt, pepper, sauce and savory.

Preparation.

Chop bread crumbs finely with pork and butter, add salt, pepper, sauce and savory to taste. Break in two or three eggs to make it the right consistency. Fill both the breast and body, and sew up.

OATMEAL MILLS.

THE OGILVIE FLOUR MILLS COMPANY, LIMITED.

WINNIPEG, MANITOBA.

SIDE DISHES

MACARONI AND OYSTERS.

Materials.

12 sticks Macaroni.
Bread or cracker crumbs.
Oysters.
Salt, pepper and butter.

Preparation.

Break the macaroni in small pieces and boil in salted water twenty minutes, or until soft. Line a baking dish with the crumbs, and put in a layer of macaroni, then one of oysters, season to taste with salt, pepper and butter. Add another layer of macaroni and so on alternately until the dish is full, moisten with milk, cover the top with crumbs and bake until the oysters are done.

CREAMED CABBAGE.

Materials.

2 cups cold cabbage, chopped.
1 tablespoon butter.
2 tablespoons Ogilvie's Royal Household.
2 cups hot milk.
1 teaspoon salt.
1 teaspoon pepper.
Cracker crumbs.

Preparation.

Melt the butter in a saucepan, add the flour, stir quickly until smooth, then add the hot milk gradually, stir until it thickens, add salt and pepper, pour over the cabbage, cover with crumbs moistened with melted butter, and brown in the oven.

OYSTER PATTIES.

Materials.

Puff paste.
Oysters.
Pepper.
Salt.
Cracker crumbs.

Preparation.

Line pattie pans with puff paste. Fill with oysters, little bits of butter, and the oyster liquor, to which a little water has been added, season with salt and pepper, cover with finely rolled cracker crumbs and bake only long enough to cook the paste.

Recipe for paste given elsewhere.

CHICKEN CROQUETTES.

Materials.

2 tablespoons butter.
2 eggs.
4 cups cold mashed potatoes.
4 cups chicken.
Pepper.
Salt.

Preparation.

To the potatoes add the butter, and beaten yolks of eggs, pepper and salt to taste. Place on stove and stir until warm. Chop some pieces of cold chicken, very fine, season to taste. Take some of the potato and form in little oval cakes in the palm of the hand, place teaspoon of chicken in centre and roll the potatoes around it. Fry in hot butter until a light brown, or bake half an hour and serve hot.

ESCALLOPED OYSTERS.

Materials.

Cracker crumbs.
Oysters.
Butter.
Pepper and salt.
1 cup rich milk.

Preparation.

Sprinkle the bottom of baking dish with the cracker crumbs and put in a layer of oysters, sprinkle with bits of butter and a little pepper and salt, now another layer of crumbs and oysters and so on until the dish is full, finishing with a layer of crumbs. On top of this pour the milk and bake from one-half to three-quarters of an hour.

CHICKEN RAMEKINS.

Materials.

> White meat of raw chicken.
> ½ teaspoon soda.
> ½ cup cream.
> 2 eggs.
> Salt and pepper.

Preparation.

Add soda to the cream, set on stove and add the meat chopped very fine, let boil for five minutes and remove, when cool add the beaten yolks of the eggs, season well with salt and pepper, then add the beaten whites, stir lightly, turn into buttered ramekin dishes and bake in a hot oven. Serve immediately.

CHEESE STRAWS.

Materials.

> 1 cup grated cheese.
> 1 cup Ogilvie's Royal Household.
> ½ teaspoon salt.
> 2 tablespoons butter.
> Pinch Cayenne pepper.

Preparation.

Mix thoroughly the cheese, flour, salt, pepper and butter, add enough cold water so that the paste can be rolled out thin, cut in strips seven inches long and half an inch wide, put in tins and bake in a quick oven for ten minutes.

POTATO CROQUETTES.

Materials.

2 cups hot potatoes (mashed)
1 tablespoon butter.
¼ teaspoon white pepper.
½ teaspoon celery salt.
1 egg.
Bread crumbs.
Onion juice (if desired).

Preparation.

Mix all but the egg and beat very light. When slightly cool add the yolk of the egg. Mould or shape into rolls, and roll in fine bread crumbs, dip in beaten white of egg, roll in crumbs again and fry in smoking hot lard one minute.

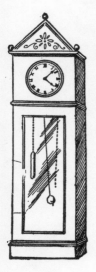

CODFISH A LA MODE.

Materials.

2 cups mashed potato (cold).
2 tablespoons butter.
2 cups milk.
2 eggs (beaten).
1 cup codfish (previously cooked).
Salt and pepper.

Preparation.

Mix potato with butter, milk and eggs, pepper and salt to taste. Add the codfish picked fine, put in buttered dish and bake thirty minutes.

SCRAMBLED EGGS.

Materials.

6 eggs.
2 tablespoons milk.
2 tablespoons water.
½ teaspoon salt.
¼ teaspoon white pepper.
2 tablespoons butter.

Preparation.

Beat the eggs without separating, add the other ingredients, mixing thoroughly. Strain the mixture. Melt the butter in a frying pan and pour in the mixture. Stir constantly until it is soft and creamy throughout. Serve at once.

This dish may be varied by the addition of any finely chopped cooked meat. If so it should be mixed with the eggs just before taking from the fire.

CODFISH BALLS.

Materials.

1 cup cooked codfish.
2 eggs.
1 cup cracker crumbs.
Fat.
1 cup mashed potatoes prepared as for the table.
Ogilvie's Royal Household.
Fried potatoes and parsley.

Preparation.

Mash the codfish very smooth. Add the potatoes and one egg well beaten, and mix thoroughly. Form in small balls about the size of an English walnut. Roll in flour then in egg and cracker crumbs and fry in deep fat. Drain, pile on a platter, garnish with fried potatoes and parsley.

BOSTON BAKED BEANS.

Materials.

4 cups beans.
¼ pound salt pork.
¼ cup molasses.
1 teaspoon mustard

Preparation.

Soak beans in cold water over night. In the morning put them into fresh cold water and simmer until soft enough to pierce with a pin, being careful not to let them boil enough to break. If you like, boil one onion with them. When soft turn into a colander, pour cold water through them and put into a bean pot. Pour boiling water over one-half pound salt pork, part fat and part lean, scrape the rind till white. Cut the rind in half-inch strips, bury the pork in the beans, leaving only the rind exposed. Mix one teaspoon of salt (more if the pork is not very salt), one teaspoon mustard with one-quarter cup molasses, and fill the cup with hot water, when well mixed pour it over the beans, add enough more water to cover them, keep covered with water until the last hour then lift the pork to the surface and let it crisp. Bake eight hours in a moderate oven.

The mustard gives the beans a delicious flavor and also renders them more wholesome.

Yellow-eyed and Lima beans are also good when baked this way.

CREAMED FISH.

Materials.

2 cups cold fish.	2 tablespoons flour.
1 cup hot milk.	½ teaspoon salt.
1 bay leaf.	¼ teaspoon white pepper.
½ teaspoon onion juice.	½ cup fine crumbs.
2 tablespoons butter.	

Preparation.

Make a sauce by creaming the flour and butter, and adding them to the hot milk. Put in a double boiler and add the salt, pepper, onion juice and bay leaf. Stir until as thick as cream. Cover the bottom of a baking dish with some of the cold fish flaked, and pour over it half of the sauce, put in another layer of fish and on that pour the remainder of the sauce.

Sprinkle with bread crumbs, dot with butter and brown in a moderately hot oven.

Any kind of cold fish may be used.

PIGS IN BLANKETS.

Materials.

Large oysters.
Thin slices of breakfast bacon.
Lemon.
Melted butter.
Pepper.
Toothpicks.
Celery.
Toast.

Preparation.

Wash and dry the oysters. Have as many strips of bacon as oysters. Place a strip of bacon lengthwise on your left hand, lay an oyster across the upper end. Begin to roll toward the tips of your fingers, when the oyster is inclosed in the bacon, skewer the latter with a small toothpick. When all prepared in this manner, sprinkle with pepper, dip in melted

butter and broil. Serve on hot toast with celery, and
garnish the platter with lemon and the white leaves
of the celery.

FRENCH OMELETTE.

Materials.

4 eggs.
5 tablespoons ice water.
½ teaspoon salt.
2 eggs (yolks).
Pinch pepper.
1 teaspoon sugar.
1 tablespoon butter (heaping).

Preparation.

Place the eggs in a bowl, beat with a fork until
they are thoroughly mixed, then strain, add the water,
salt, pepper and sugar. Melt butter in a frying pan,
pour in the egg mixture. Set over the fire for a minute,
then with a spatula separate the cooked portions and
gently move it back and forth so that the uncooked
part may come in contact with the pan. When it
becomes creamy and begins to set begin at the side of
the pan and fold the omelette over.

Turn on to a hot platter and serve immediately.

EGGS WITH CREAM DRESSING.

Materials.

2 tablespoons butter.
3 tablespoons Ogilvie's Royal Household.
1½ cups milk.
1 teaspoon salt.
Pinch pepper.
3 eggs (hard boiled).

Preparation.

Cream butter and flour, place on stove and stir
until butter is melted. Add milk, stirring all the time
till mixture is thick, add salt and pepper. Separate
the whites of the eggs from the yolks, chop the whites
fine and add to the dressing. Arrange slices of toast
on a hot platter, pour the dressing over them; force
the yolks through a ricer on to the toast and dressing,
serve hot.

PUFF OMELETTE.

Materials.

4 eggs.	6 tablespoons water.
2 eggs (yolks).	½ teaspoon salt.
Pinch pepper.	1 tablespoon butter.

Preparation.

Beat the whites of the eggs until dry, and the yolks until they are thick and of a lemon color. Add the water, salt and pepper to the yolks. Mix thoroughly and fold the whites into the yolk mixture. Put the butter in a frying an, and when hot put in the mixture. Let it stand in a moderate heat for two minutes, place in a hot oven and cook until set. Remove from the oven, cut across the centre, turn on a hot platter and serve.

NOTE.—The number of yolks should exceed the number of whites in an omelette. If this rule is observed they will be more tender, and of a looser texture.

MEAT SCALLOP.

Materials.

1 tablespoon butter.
½ teaspoon onion (minced).
1 tablespoon Ogilvie's Royal Household.
⅔ cup hot water.
1 cup cold meat (chopped).
Mashed potato.

Preparation.

Put butter and onion in a saucepan and set on stove, when hot add flour and stir until smooth, then add water and season to taste, now add meat and mix all together. Put in a baking dish and cover with a layer of mashed potatoes seasoned with salt and pepper, and wet with a little milk. Adding the beaten white of an egg will greatly improve the potato. Bake for twenty minutes or until a light brown. Serve hot.

BY ROYAL WARRANT MILLERS TO H.R.H. THE PRINCE OF WALES.

Use "Royal Household" for Pastry as well as for Bread

Do you know that "Royal Household" makes the best pastry you ever tasted? Well, it does. And you can have this best pastry just as well as the most skillful pastry cook in the land.

There is no secret about it. Use any of the recipes in this book for cake, pies, doughnuts, etc., follow the directions exactly, and you cannot fail.

The old fashioned theory of having one flour for bread and another for pastry won't "hold water" when "Royal Household" comes in the kitchen.

"ROYAL HOUSEHOLD" is a pastry flour just as much as a bread flour, and it proves this by making the best pastry just as it makes the best bread.

Try it—the right way—and see for yourself.

STEEL GRAIN ELEVATOR.   CAPACITY 750,000 BUSHELS.
THE OGILVIE FLOUR MILLS COMPANY, LIMITED,
FORT WILLIAM, ONT.

SALADS

"We should cultivate a taste for wholesome
green foods."

No absolute rule can be laid down for the making
of salads, but as the simpler ones are always acceptable,
begin with them and you will gradually become an
expert salad maker.

The one rule applying to all salads is to have them
very cold and to serve them daintily. A few of those
liked most will be found herein. You can invent many
others, for salads are nowadays made of everything
imaginable.

CHICKEN SALAD.

Materials.

1 chicken.	Lemon juice.
1 onion, sliced.	Celery.
1 bay leaf.	Mayonnaise.
6 cloves.	Whipped cream.
1 teaspoon salt.	Lettuce.
½ teaspoon white pepper	Mace.
	Capers.

Preparation.

Clean and dress the chicken. Place in boiling
water, add onion, bay leaf, cloves and mace. Bring
to a boil and let it boil five minutes. Reduce the heat
to below the boiling point, and let cook until tender.

By cooking it in this manner the dark meat will
be almost as white as the meat of the breast. When
the chicken is cold, cut in half inch cubes, removing
all the fat and skin. To each pint allow one tablespoon
lemon juice, sprinkle the latter over prepared chicken
and place on ice. When ready to serve, mix chicken

with two-thirds as much white celery cut into corresponding pieces. Dust with salt and pepper, mix the mayonnaise—Recipe elsewhere herein—with whipped cream to taste, pour over the salad. Serve on lettuce leaves and garnish the dish with the white leaves of the celery. Sprinkle the top of the salad with capers.

Duck, turkey or sweetbreads may be substituted for chicken and give—

>DUCK SALAD,
>
>TURKEY SALAD and
>
>SWEETBREAD SALAD.

MAYONNAISE.

Materials.

2 raw egg yolks.	Yolks of 2 boiled eggs.
2 cups olive oil.	2 teaspoons salt.
1 teaspoon made mustard.	½ teaspoon pepper.
	2 tablespoons vinegar.
1 teaspoon lemon juice	Sugar.

Preparation.

Place mixing bowl in a larger one full of cracked ice. Put the yolk of both raw and boiled eggs in the bowl. Drop in a little oil and rub to a cream. Add mustard, salt, pepper, and a pinch of sugar. Now add the oil, drop by drop, beating all the time until the mixture is thick and stiff enough to keep its shape and has a shiny appearance. Thin it by addition of the vinegar, a drop at a time, until the dressing is of the proper consistency. Add the lemon juice and just before using, the stiffly-beaten whites of the eggs. Keep this dressing very cold.

If a mild dressing is wanted omit the mustard and pepper. For fruit salad omit the mustard and use the sugar instead.

For a still milder dressing omit mustard and pepper, use only half of the oil, and cream instead.

SALMON SALAD.

Materials.

1 can salmon.
1 cup chopped celery.
2 eggs (hard boiled).
1 cup salad dressing.
Olives (Pitted).
Lettuce leaves.

Preparation.

Pour off oil from the salmon, remove bones and skin, mix lightly with a fork. Add the celery and egg chopped fine, then the salad dressing. Garnish with olives and lettuce leaves.

WALDORF SALAD.

Materials.

1 cup apples (peeled and chopped).
1 cup celery (chopped).
½ cup walnuts (chopped).
Salad dressing.
Lettuce leaves

Preparation.

Mix apples, celery and walnuts with salad dressing. Garnish with lettuce leaves. Do not make until ready to use, as apples turn dark.

SALAD DRESSING.

Materials.

4 tablespoons butter.
1 tablespoon Ogilvie's Royal Household.
1 tablespoon celery salt.
1 tablespoon mustard.
1 tablespoon sugar.
1 cup milk.
½ cup vinegar, or juice of one large lemon.
3 eggs.
Pinch Cayenne pepper.

Preparation.

Melt butter in saucepan, add the flour and stir until smooth, being careful not to brown, add milk and

let come to a boil. Place saucepan in another of hot
water, beat the eggs, salt, pepper, sugar and mustard
together and add the vinegar or lemon. Stir this
until it boils and thickens like soft custard which will
require about five minutes.

POTATO SALAD.

Materials.

6 cups of potatoes (cooked).
1 small onion.
Pepper.
Salt.

Preparation.

Chop potatoes and onion fine, add salt and pepper
to taste. Mix with boiled salad dressing, as follows:

BOILED SALAD DRESSING.

Materials.

3 tablespoons butter.
6 tablespoons vinegar.
3 eggs.
6 tablespoons milk.
1 teaspoon mixed mustard.
½ teaspoon salt.
½ teaspoon celery salt.
¼ teaspoon pepper.

Preparation.

Put vinegar and butter into porcelain or granite
pan, and place on stove. When butter is melted take
off and cool. Beat the eggs until light, add mustard,
salt, celery salt, pepper and milk. Pour this into the
cooled mixture, set on stove, stirring constantly from
the bottom of the pan. When it begins to thicken
take off at once and stir until smooth.

BEET SALAD.

Materials.

½ doz. beets.
Vinegar.
Cucumbers (chopped).
Celery.
Lettuce leaves.
Parsley.

88

Preparation.

Boil the beets, peel while warm, cut off the stem ends and scoop out the centre, cover with vinegar and let stand over night. When required, fill the beets with equal parts of cucumbers and celery chopped fine. Place each one upon a lettuce leaf, pour over it a boiled dressing and sprinkle with parsley cut fine.

This is very nice.

CABBAGE SALAD.

Materials.

½ cup vinegar.	1 egg.
1 tablespoon butter.	½ cup sweet milk.
1 tablespoon mustard.	½ head cabbage.
1 tablespoon brown sugar.	Pepper and salt.

Preparation.

Put vinegar and butter in a dish and set on stove, let come to a boil. After mixing thoroughly add the mustard, brown sugar, milk and well beaten egg. Stir in slowly with the vinegar until it boils. Chop the cabbage fine, salt and pepper to taste, put in the dressing and let come to a boil. When cold it is ready to serve.

BANANA AND ORANGE SALAD.

Materials.

6 oranges.
3 bananas.
½ lemon (juice).
½ cup pineapple juice.
½ cup sugar.
1 egg (white).

Preparation.

Peel and cut in small pieces four of the oranges and the bananas. Mix the lemon juice, sugar, and beaten egg with the juice of the two remaining oranges. Bring to a boil, strain and pour over the fruit, add the pineapple juice last. Serve cold.

BY ROYAL WARRANT, MILLERS TO H.R.H. THE PRINCE OF WALES.

THE woman who has not strength of mind enough to break away from the old traditions and use

"Royal Household"

for both bread and pastry, will never know what deliciously light, flaky pastry it will make.

It goes without saying that it makes the best Bread.

HOW ROYAL HOUSEHOLD IS DELIVERED TO CUSTOMERS.

WITH A CHAFING-DISH

"The chief pleasure in eating does not consist in costly seasoning or exquisite flavour, but in yourself."
—*Horace*.

The use of the chafing dish is, contrary to general opinion, far older than our present civilization. It reaches in some form back into the times of the ancient Greeks and Romans.

As used at present, alcohol is the fuel for the lamp attached to it, and a tray is desirable to protect table-cloths and table from alcohol and fire. The cap covering the opening through which the lamp is filled, should be kept in place after filling it. Otherwise controlling the flame is hardly possible.

A chafing-dish needs to be watched carefully from a chair with a high seat to make its use comfortable. For the benefit of the comparatively few who can and care to indulge in its use, the following recipes are presented.

WELSH RAREBIT.

Materials.

½ lb. cheese.	2 teaspoons butter.
½ cup cream or milk.	1 teaspoon salt.
2 teaspoons mustard.	½ pound fresh crackers.

Preparation.

Grate cheese and put in a chafing dish, stir constantly until melted. Then add cream or milk, slightly warmed, and stir until smooth. Mix mustard, salt, pepper and beaten egg, and add to the above, when it becomes thick, pour over toasted crackers.

CREAMED OYSTERS.

Materials.

1 dozen oysters.
2 eggs (yolks).
½ cup cream.
1 teaspoon butter.
Salt and pepper to taste.

Preparation.

Chop oysters quite fine, season with salt and pepper. Melt the butter and add the oyster mince. Let simmer a few minutes then add yolks of eggs beaten with cream. When eggs set, serve on saltine.

OYSTER A LA NEWBURG.

Materials.

2 cups oysters.
1 tablespoon butter.
3 eggs (yolks).
½ cup cream.
Salt and pepper to taste.

Preparation.

Drain and pick out pieces of shell from oysters. Melt the butter and add salt, pepper and oysters, cook gently for six minutes. Beat the yolks of the eggs with cream, and pour over the oysters, and as soon as creamy serve.

CREAMED SHRIMPS WITH GREEN PEAS.

Materials.

1½ cup cream.
2 tablespoons butter.
2 small cans shrimps.
1 can French peas.
1 tablespoon flour.
2 eggs.
½ pound crackers.

Preparation.

Heat cream until hot, add butter and flour creamed together, stir until smooth, then add shrimps, beaten eggs and peas, when thoroughly hot serve on toast or toasted crackers. Salmon may be used in the place of shrimps if desired.

VENETIAN EGGS.

Materials.

1 can tomatoes.
1 pound cheese.
5 eggs (yolks).
1 small onion.
1 tablespoon butter.

Pinch Cayenne.
Pepper and salt to taste.

Preparation.

Put butter in chafing dish, add the grated onion and cook five minutes. Put in the cheese cut in small pieces, cook until melted, add the tomato juice which has been heated and strained, then the well beaten yolks of the eggs, pepper, salt and Cayenne.

LOBSTER A LA NEWBURG.

Materials.

2 cups cream.
2 eggs.
2 tablespoons butter.
2 cups lobster.

1 tablespoon flour.
$\frac{1}{4}$ teaspoon mustard
Salt, red pepper.
Worcestershire sauce.

Preparation.

Put cream in a chafing dish, when hot add butter and flour creamed, and stir until thoroughly smooth. Add lobster broken in fine pieces and let come to a boil, put in beaten egg, season with salt and pepper and the mustard mixed with Worcestershire sauce. When thoroughly cooked pour over crackers or toast. A cup of green peas may be added if desired.

PRESERVES & PICKLES

CANNED RASPBERRIES.

Materials.

Fresh raspberries.
Sugar.

Preparation.

Use one cup of sugar to two cups of berries. Fill cans alternately with berries and sugar, place in a boiler on the stove, (if using glass fruit jars put sticks under them to keep from breaking). fill the boiler with cold water nearly to the top of the cans. As the berries settle fill again with berries and sugar until the juice fills the cans and is red. Then put covers on and tighten down, let cook for five minutes. Remove from water and place on a board out of the draft·

ORANGE MARMALADE.

Materials.

6 oranges.
3 lemons.
10 cups water.
10 cups sugar.

Preparation.

Slice oranges and lemons fine, remove seeds and soak twenty-four hours in the water. Boil for one hour, add sugar and boil another hour, or until it jellies. Put in tumblers and cover.

SPICE JELLY.

Materials.

4 pounds apples.
1½ tablespoons whole cloves.
2 tablespoons cassia.
Sugar.

96

Preparation.

Cut the apples in small pieces, and cover with vinegar and water, about half of each, tie spices in a bag and boil with apples, drip and add cup of sugar to cup of juice, cook until it jellies, then remove spice bag and put in jars.

GINGER PEARS.

Materials.

4 cups preserved ginger.	8 lbs. pears.
Juice of five lemons.	6 lbs. sugar.
Rind of five lemons.	2 oranges.
Hot water.	

Preparation.

Cut the ginger in thin slices. Press the juice out of the lemons and oranges, and cut their rind into shreds. Peel the pears and cut them crosswise in the slices. Add enough hot water to dissolve the sugar, when hot add lemon and orange juice, ginger, lemon rind, and orange peel, lastly the pears and cook slowly for three hours. Place in pint fruit jars and seal. Keep in a cool dry place.

PRESERVED PEACHES.

Preparation.

Pare peaches and place in steamer over boiling water, cover tightly; an earthen plate placed in steamer will preserve the juices which may be added to the syrup. Let steam until they can be pierced with a fork. Make a syrup of one-half pound of sugar to a pint of water, put fruit in cans, when full pour over it the hot syrup. This rule is excellent for all large fruits.

CHOW-CHOW.

Materials.

1 peck green tomatoes	6 cups (3 pounds) brown sugar.
½ peck ripe tomatoes.	
12 onions.	1 tablespoon black pepper.
3 heads cabbage.	1 tablespoon ground mustard.
1 cup salt.	
1 cup grated horse radish.	1 tablespoon celery seed.
	Vinegar.

97

Preparation.

Chop and mix the tomatoes, onions, cabbage and red pepper. Sprinkle salt over them and let stand for twenty-four hours, then drain, put in a kettle with the grated horse radish, sugar, black pepper, mustard, and celery seed, cover all with vinegar and boil until clear.

CANNED CORN.

Preparation.

Grate corn from the cobs, put cobs on to boil in cold water to cover; boil twenty minutes and strain, mix corn and corn water in the proportions of four bowls of water to two of corn and two tablespoons sugar, cook on top of stove until it swells, fill glass jars, put rubbers and covers in place and cook again in a kettle of hot water one hour, tighten the covers and wrap in paper. Keep in a cool dark place.

STRING BEANS CANNED.

Preparation.

String and break, cover with hot water and cook two hours. Fill glass jars full of beans with the water they have been cooking in, place rubbers and covers on, screw nearly tight and cook one hour longer in a kettle of hot water, tighten covers, wrap in paper and keep in a cool dark place.

TOMATO PICKLES.

Materials.

1 peck green tomatoes.	¼ pound whole mustard.
6 large onions.	2 tablespoons cinnamon.
1 cup salt.	2 tablespoons allspice.
8 cups water.	2 tablespoons cloves.
4 cups vinegar.	2 tablespoons ginger.
2 pounds brown sugar.	1 teaspoon Cayenne.

Preparation.

Slice the tomatoes with onions, sprinkle the salt over them and let stand over night, drain off in the morning and put in a porcelain kettle with the water and vinegar, let the mixture boil fifteen minutes. Drain off, cover with vinegar, add the other ingredients, and boil fifteen minutes longer, if preferred the dark spices may be put in a bag.

SWEET PICKLES.

Materials.

    4 cups vinegar.
    4 cups brown sugar.
    2 tablespoons whole cloves.
    Allspice and cinnamon.
    7 lbs. fruit, watermelon rinds, apples, ripe cucumbers (seeded).

Preparation.

Boil fruit until it can be pierced with a straw, put in cans, boil other ingredients a few minutes, pour over fruit while hot, and set away.

CUCUMBER PICKLES.

Materials.

    100 small cucumbers.
    1 cup sugar.
    1 tablespoon mixed spice.
    1 small red pepper.
    4 cups white wine vinegar.
    Small piece alum.

Preparation.

Pour hot salt brine over pickles and let stand over night. In the morning rinse pickles in clear water Take enough vinegar and water (one part vinegar, two parts water) to cover pickles, bring to a boil, drop in pickles and let scald five minutes, drain and put in cans. Have ready the white wine vinegar and sugar, mixed spices, red pepper cut in small pieces, and alum, let come to a boil, pour over the pickles in cans and seal.

THE big, snowy loaves of bread that "ROYAL HOUSEHOLD" Flour turns out, with their brown, crisp, crackling crusts, are but a hint of the deliciously light, flaky pastry you can make with it.

Follow directions given in this Cook Book.

Use "Royal Household"

AND

GOOD BREAD AND GOOD PASTRY IS ASSURED.

HEAD OFFICE:
OGILVIE'S ROYAL HOUSEHOLD FLOUR,
MONTREAL.

FRUIT JELLY.

Materials.

¾ box gelatine.
2 cups cold water.
2 cups boiling water.
1 lemon (juice)
3 oranges.

2 bananas.
½ lb. Malaga grapes.
6 figs.
10 English walnuts.

Preparation.

Dissolve the gelatine in cold water, then add boiling water and lemon juice. Cut fruit and walnuts in small pieces, remove seeds from grapes and stir all into the gelatine. Turn into a mould, when hard serve with whipped cream.

SOFT CUSTARD.

Materials.

2 cups milk.
4 eggs.
1 cup sugar.
Vanilla flavoring.

Preparation.

Beat the yolks of the eggs with the sugar and stir into the boiling milk, continue stirring until cooked when cool flavor with vanilla. Beat the whites of the eggs to a stiff froth and put on top of custard either in a large dish or custard glasses.

103

ORANGE PUDDING.

Materials.

5 oranges.
1 cup sugar (heaping).
2 cups milk.
3 eggs.
1 tablespoon flour.
1 tablespoon sugar.

Preparation.

Select good sweet juicy oranges, peel and cut in thin slices, taking out the seeds and pour the sugar over them. Let the milk get boiling hot by setting it in a vessel of boiling water. Add the yolks of the eggs well beaten and the flour made smooth in a little cold milk, stir all the time and as soon as thickened pour over the fruit. Beat the whites of the eggs to a stiff froth, add the sugar and spread it on for frosting, set in oven a few minutes to harden. Serve cold.

Substitute berries or any fruit you prefer. Peaches are very nice this way.

SPANISH CREAM.

Materials.

4 cups milk.
½ box gelatine.
4 eggs.
⅔ cup sugar.

Preparation.

Soak the gelatine in the milk over night. In the morning add the sugar to beaten yolks of the eggs, stir into the milk and gelatine, continue stirring and add the whites of the eggs beaten to a stiff froth. Flavor as desired and turn into moulds, set where it will keep cool and serve as you would ice cream.

CHOCOLATE CUSTARD.

Materials.

3 cups milk.
2 ounces sweet chocolate.
½ cup sugar.
4 eggs.

Preparation.

Put the milk on the stove in a double boiler and while it is heating grate the chocolate into a bowl. Add the sugar, and yolks of the eggs, beat to a cream. When the milk begins to wrinkle over the top, gradually pour it into the bowl with the mixture of eggs, chocolate and sugar, stirring it briskly to prevent lumping, then turn the entire mixture back into the double boiler, set in the hot water again, and let it cook until it is as thick cream. After it has cooled pour into a glass dish. When cold and ready to serve cover the top with whipped cream.

STRAWBERRY CHARLOTTE.

Materials.

4 cups milk.
6 eggs.
¾ cup sugar.
Sponge cake (recipe elsewhere).
Sweet cream.
Strawberries.

Preparation.

Make a soft custard with the milk, yolks of eggs and sugar, flavor to taste. (Directions given under "Soft Custard"). Line a glass dish with slices of sponge cake dipped in sweet cream, then a layer of strawberries sweetened to taste, then a layer of cake and berries as before. When the custard is cold pour over the whole. Beat the whites of the eggs to a stiff froth, add a little sugar and spread over the top. Decorate with berries.

BLANC MANGE.

Materials.

4 cups milk.
1 cup sugar.
Small handful Irish moss.
Lemon flavoring.

Preparation.

Wash the moss thoroughly, put in a pail and pour the milk over it. Set the pail closely covered in a kettle of boiling water, let stand until the moss thickens the milk, then strain through a fine sieve, add sugar and flavor to taste. Wet the moulds in cold water, pour in the blanc mange, and set in a cool place. When quite firm it is ready for use. Loosen the edges from the moulds and turn out on a china or glass plates Serve with sugar and cream.

TAPIOCA CREAM

Materials.

2 cups milk.
2 tablespoons minute tapioca.
½ cup sugar.
2 eggs.
Pinch of salt.

Preparation.

Cook the milk, tapioca and sugar for about ten minutes in a double boiler. Add beaten yolks of the eggs, and the pinch of salt, then the whites beaten stiff. When cool pour over canned peaches, cut in a small pieces.

Serve with whipped cream if desired.

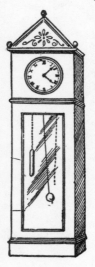

ICE CREAM & SHERBETS

"Then farewell heat and welcome frost."
—*Merchant of Venice.*

FREEZING.

Pour the chilled cream into the freezer. Place into the pail and pack with ice nearly to the top. Sprinkle coarse salt uniformly on the ice as you pack it into the bucket. Cover and fasten the can and turn it slowly until it becomes difficult to turn. Open the can and remove the dasher. Scrape the cream from the sides, mix until smooth, close the can and drain off the brine. Add fresh ice and salt, covering the entire can. Wrap a blanket around the freezer and let it stand two hours.

In very hot weather renew the salt and ice three times, keep the blanket cold and wet with the brine from the freezer.

ORANGE ICE.

Materials.

4 cups water.
2 cups sugar.
2 cups orange juice.
½ cup lemon juice.

Grated rind of one orange.
Grated rind of one lemon.

Preparation.

Make a syrup of the sugar and water. Boil fifteen minutes, add the orange and lemon juice, the orange peel, and lemon rind.

Freeze (according to directions elsewhere herein) and serve in glasses.

STRAWBERRY ICE CREAM.

Materials.

4 cups cream.
4 cups strawberries.
8 cups sugar.

Preparation.

Mash the strawberries and sugar together, and let them stand one or two hours. Add the cream, rub through a strainer into the freezer and freeze as directed elsewhere.

VANILLA ICE CREAM.

Materials.

3 cups cream.	1 cup sugar (heaping).
1 cup milk.	1 tablespoon vanilla.
2 eggs.	

Preparation.

Beat the eggs, mix altogether and freeze as directed elsewhere. Any other flavoring may be substituted for vanilla if preferred.

LEMON SHERBET.

Materials.

4 lemons.
2 cups sugar.
4 cups boiling water.

Preparation.

Shave off the peel from two lemons in thin, wafer-like parings, being careful to take none of the lighter colored rind below the oil cells. Put the parings in a bowl, add the boiling water and let it stand ten minutes closely covered. Cut the lemons in halves, remove the seeds, squeeze out the juice, and add with the sugar to the water. Add more sugar if needed, when cold strain it through a fine strainer into a can, and freeze.

ORANGE SHERBET.

Materials.

3 cups sugar.
6 cups water.
10 oranges (juice only).

Preparation.

Boil sugar and water together twenty-five minutes, add orange juice, strain and freeze.

CAFE PARFAIT.

Materials.
>   3 cups cream.
>   ½ cup strong coffee (clear and cold).
>   1 cup sugar.

Preparation.

Whip the cream stiff, adding sugar and coffee a little at a time while whipping.   Put in a mould and pack quickly in fine ice and salt ; in the winter, snow is better than ice.   This should always be ready before the cream is whipped.

STRAWBERRY SHERBET.

Materials.
>   3 cups strawberry juice.
>   2 cups sugar.
>   3 cups water.
>   2 lemons (juice only).

Preparation.

Boil water and sugar together for twenty-five minutes, add lemon and strawberry juice, strain and freeze.   Raspberry Sherbet is made in the same way.

PINEAPPLE SHERBET.

Materials.

2 cups of fresh or	1 lemon (juice).
1 can grated pineapple.	8 cups milk.
3 cups sugar.	1 tablespoon vanilla.

Preparation,

Mix and freeze as ice cream.   Strawberries or any kind of fruit can be used instead of Pineapple.

PINE APPLE ICE

Materials.

4 cups water.	4 cups ice water.
2 cups sugar.	1 can grated pineapple.
Juice of six lemons.	

Preparation.

Make a syrup of the water and sugar, boil for fifteen minutes. Add the pineapple and lemon juice. Cool and add ice water. Freeze until mushy, using half ice and half salt.

ROMAN PUNCH.

Materials.

8 cups pineapple ice.	4 eggs (whites).
1 cup Jamaica rum.	2 tablespoons vanilla.
½ lb. sugar.	2 cups champagne.
	1 cup water.

Preparation.

Put the sugar in a saucepan, add one cup water. Boil until it will form a ball when dropped in water and rolled between the thumb and finger. Beat the whites of the eggs very stiff and gradually add to them the hot syrup, stirring until cold. Mix the rum and vanilla with the pineapple ice and beat in the egg mixture, whip in the champagne and serve immediately.

WILD GRAPE WINE.

Preparation.

Remove the grapes from the stem, bruise. To one gallon of grapes put on a gallon of boiling water, let stand one week without stirring, then strain, to each gallon of juice allow four pounds of white sugar, put in a wide mouth stone jar, when done fermenting, strain, and bottle. If filtered before bottling it will be much clearer. It improves by keeping.

RASPBERRY SHRUB.

Preparation.

Four quarts red raspberries to one quart vinegar, let stand four days, strain. To each pint of juice add one pound granulated sugar, boil twenty minutes, bottle, and keep in a dry cool place.

INVALID DISHES

" Such dainties to them, their health it might hurt :
Its like sending them ruffles when wanting a shirt."
Goldsmith

The greatest weight is to be attached to the preparation of food for the sick. Oftentimes the diet is of more importance than the drug. Entire wholesomeness of food, the best preparation possible, and prompt and dainty service are necessary requisites.

Do not consult the patient as to the menu, for the various surprises will help to tickle the appetite.

First prepare the tray with a spotless cloth or napkin folded just to cover; then select the smallest, prettiest dishes from the sideboard, being careful to place everything in an orderly and convenient manner. Serve hot food on hot dishes, cold food on cold dishes.

For feverish patients, cold water mixed with fruit juices is refreshing and beneficial.

When raw eggs are ordered, a warm lemonade into which the well-beaten egg is stirred makes an agreeable change.

Care should be taken that the lemonade is not hot enough to cook the egg.

ALMOND SOUP.

Materials.

½ lb. almonds.
2 cups milk.
2 tablespoons sugar.
½ teaspoon salt.
2 cups hot milk.

Preparation.

Blanch the almonds and pound them in a mortar, gradually adding the two cups milk. When pounded to a smooth paste, and all of the milk has been used, strain it by squeezing through a piece of cheesecloth. To the scalded milk add sugar and salt, now add to the almond mixture and bring to the boiling point. Serve hot.

BROILED BEEF JUICE.

Materials.

2 lbs. lean steak from the top of the round.
Salt, pepper.

Preparation.

Remove any visible fat from the steak, broil over a brisk fire for four minutes, turning it frequently Cut in pieces about one inch square, and gash each piece two or three times. Place in a meat press and squeeze the juice into a hot cup. Season to taste, and serve hot.

CHICKEN BROTH.

Materials.

¼ lb. fowl.
2 quarts water.
Seasoning.

Preparation.

Joint the fowl and skin it, removing all visible fat. Break the bones, place in a saucepan and pour the water over it. Let stand one hour. Bring slowly to the boiling point and simmer for three hours. Strain, cool, remove all fat and season to taste. This may be served either hot or cold.

BARLEY WATER.

Materials.

2 tablespoons pearl barley.
4 cups water.

Preparation.

Put barley over the fire in cold water, let come to a boil and cook five minutes, then drain off the water and rinse the barley in cold water. Return it to the fire, add one quart of water. Bring it to a boil and simmer until reduced one-half. It may be sweetened and flavored if desired.

OATMEAL GRUEL.

Materials.
½ cup oatmeal.
6 cups boiling water.
1 teaspoon salt.
Sugar.
Cream.

Preparation.
Add salt to the boiling water, stir in the oatmeal and cook for two and one-half hours in a double boiler. Remove from the fire and strain. When preparing it for a patient, use half a cup of the gruel mixed with half a cup of thin cream, two tablespoons boiling water and sugar to taste.

A pinch of nutmeg or cinnamon is also sometimes added. Other gruels are also prepared in the same manner.

CHICKEN CUSTARD.

Materials.
½ cup bread crumbs.
2 eggs (yolks).
Pinch of celery salt.
1 cup milk.
2 tablespoons chopped breast of chicken.
Pinch of salt.

Preparation.
Take the crumbs from the centre of a stale loaf and add to them the chicken. Beat the yolks until well mixed, add to them the salt, celery salt and milk. Pour this over the other ingredients, mixing thoroughly. Fill a custard cup with the mixture, place in a pan of hot water and bake in a moderate oven until set. Serve hot.

FLAXSEED LEMONADE.

Materials.
2 tablespoons flaxseed.
4 cups boiling water.
1 cup sugar.
Grated rind and juice of three lemons.

113

Preparation.

Blanch the flaxseed, add boiling water and let it simmer for three quarters of an hour, then add sugar and lemon rind. Let it stand for fifteen minutes. Strain and add lemon juice. Serve either hot or cold For a bad cough, take a teaspoon every half hour.

RICE WATER.

Materials.

2 tablespoons rice.   1 teaspoon salt.
4 cups boiling water.   Flavoring, sugar.

Preparation.

Blanch the rice, drain and add the boiling water. Cook for an hour and a quarter, keeping it simmering only. Then strain, add the salt and use when needed. Sweetening and flavoring to taste, may be added if desired. Rice water is also used to dilute milk, and is sometimes combined with chicken broth.

WINE WHEY.

Materials.

2 cups milk.
1 cup sherry wine.

Preparation.

Heat the milk to a boiling point, the add the sherry. Bring it again to the boiling point and strain through cheesecloth.

EGGNOG.

Materials.

2 eggs.
2 tablespoons sugar.
2 tablespoons wine or brandy.
1 cup cream or milk.

Preparation.

Beat the egg until light and creamy, add the sugar and beat again, then the wine or brandy, lastly the cream or milk, put in freezer until half frozen.

"Sweets to the Sweet."—Hamlet.

CHOCOLATE CARAMELS.

Materials.

> 3 cups white sugar.
> 1 cup milk or cream.
> ½ cup butter.
> 4 ounces unsweetened chocolate.

Preparation.

Mix all together and let boil without much stirring until it will be brittle when dropped into cold water, then turn on buttered shoal pan and when it begins to harden, mark off so it will break into squares.

WALNUT CREAMS.

Materials.

> 1 egg (white).
> Powdered sugar.
> Walnuts.
> Flavoring

Preparation.

Mix egg with sugar to make it stiff so as to roll in little balls, then on each side place one-half a walnut.

MAPLE PUFFS.

Materials.

½ lb. maple sugar.	½ cup chopped figs.
½ lb. brown sugar.	½ cup chopped citron.
2 eggs (whites).	½ cup raisins.
1 cup English walnuts.	½ cup water.

Preparation.

Boil sugar and water until they spin a heavy thread. Beat the whites of the eggs very stiff, gradually add the hot syrup to whites of the eggs, beating all the time. When the mixture begins to stiffen add the other ingredients. Beat until it will hold its shape.

Place by tablespoons on greased paper and let stand until stiff.

FONDANT.

Materials.

2 cups sugar.
½ cup water.
Flavoring.

Preparation.

Stir until sugar is dissolved, then remove the spoon and boil steadily without disturbing, until the soft ball stage is reached. Take from the fire and cool at once. Add flavor and beat with a spoon or knife until the mass turns creamy and becomes firm enough to mould.

VELVET KISSES.

Materials.

1 cup molasses.
3 cups white sugar.
1 cup water (boiling).
½ cup butter (melted).
3 tablespoons vinegar.
½ teaspoon cream tartar.
¼ teaspoon soda.
Vanilla.

Preparation.

Put molasses, sugar, water, and vinegar in granite kettle, when boiling add cream tartar, boil until mixture becomes brittle in cold water, stir constantly during the last part of the cooking. When nearly done add soda and melted butter, cook until brittle, cool and pull. While pulling, flavor. Cut in small pieces and do up in oil papers.

116

SMITH COLLEGE FUDGE.

Materials.

    1 cup brown sugar.
    ¼ cup butter.
    ½ cup cream.
    1 cup white sugar.
    ¼ cup molasses.
    2 squares Baker's chocolate.
    ½ teaspoon vanilla.

Preparation,

    Mix sugar, butter, cream, molasses and chocolate together and cook until it forms a heavy thread, take from fire, add vanilla, stir constantly until the mass thickens. Pour in buttered pans.

CHOCOLATE DROPS.

Materials.

    2 cups white sugar.
    ½ cup water.
    Vanilla.
    Huyler's chocolate.

Preparation.

    Boil sugar and water without stirring until it ropes, pour on cold platter, let it cool about five minutes, beat until it creams, while beating add vanilla. Make into balls and place on greased paper. Melt chocolate and keep warm in pan of hot water. Pick up balls on knitting needle and dip in chocolate. Ready to serve in twenty minutes

CREAM PEPPERMINTS.

Materials.

    2 cups sugar.
    ½ cup water.
    1 tablespoon glucose.
    Oil of peppermint.

Preparation.

Boil sugar, water and glucose until it forms a soft substance when dropped in cold water ; take from the fire and when lukewarm flavor with peppermint and beat until thick.

Drop on buttered paper with teaspoon

MOLASSES CANDY.

Materials.

1 cup molasses.
3 cups sugar.
½ cup water.
1 teaspoon cream tartar.

Preparation.

Mix sugar and cream tartar together, add molasses and water, and stir until sugar is dissolved, then boil without stirring until it hardens in cold water. Turn into buttered pan; when cool, work and cut in sticks.

MAPLE CREAM.

Materials.

1 pound maple sugar.
⅛ teaspoon cream tartar.
½ cup milk.

Preparation.

Boil all together until when dropped in very cold water it will form a soft ball, then beat until creamy.

BROWN SUGAR CANDY.

Materials.

2 cups brown sugar.
½ cup milk or cream.
Butter (size of walnut).
Walnuts.
Vanilla.

118

Preparation.

Boil until it forms a soft lump, when dropped into water remove from fire, beat until it begins to thicken, then add one cup chopped walnuts and vanilla to taste, pour into buttered dish.

PEANUT CRISP.

Materials.

2 cups white sugar.
1 cup peanuts.

Preparation.

Put sugar in pan over hot fire and stir until melted. Pour the liquid over peanuts which have been placed in a buttered dish.

USEFUL HINTS

CHINA CEMENT.

Broken china may be mended by making a light paste out of the white of an egg and flour, cleaning the broken edges from dust, and spreading with the paste and holding the parts while wet, wiping off all that oozes out. It must be held or fastened in position until dry.

RUST STAINS ON WHITE GOODS.

Lemon juice and salt will remove rust stains from linen or muslin without affecting the goods. Let the sun shine on the goods after having moistened the spots with the mixture—two or three applications may be necessary.

GRASS STAINS ON CLOTHING.

Should be saturated with alcohol for a little time, then wash in clear water.

REMOVING STARCH FROM IRONS.

Should starch cling to your iron while using it, sprinkle some salt on a piece of brown paper and rub the iron on it.

TO SOFTEN BOOTS AND SHOES.

Rub your boots and shoes well with castor oil and let them stand twelve hours. This will keep them from cracking and make them yielding and soft.

KEROSENE OIL.

Coal oil will help the housekeeper out of many difficulties. A spoonful of Kerosene added to a kettle of very hot water will make windows, looking-glasses and picture glasses bright and clear. Use a small clean cloth, wring it dry and rub it over the glass after wiping down the framework with an oiled cloth. Then proceed to the next window and treat it similarly on both sides. After that go back to the first one and wipe it dry with a large clean cloth No real polishing is required and the windows or glass will look clean and shiny.

Kerosene will clean your hands better than anything else after blacking a range or stove. Pour a little in the water, wash your hands in it, then wash in tepid water, and finally in hot water with plenty of soap, and using a stiff nail brush. Finish by rubbing the hands with lemon and glycerine.

When your kitchen sink is rusty rub it over with kerosene.

Squeaky shoes are cured by dipping the soles in kerosene. Use enough to reach the top of the soles without reaching the upper leather.

The white spots appearing in the spring on the lining of your refrigerator will disappear if you rub the zinc with kerosene. Leave the refrigerator open several hours, then wash with water, soap and some ammonia. The refrigerator will then be clean and sweet, all spots will have disappeared.

TO DESTROY INSECTS.

Insects may be destroyed with hot alum. Put in hot water and let boil until the alum is dissolved. Apply hot with a brush and all creeping things are instantly destroyed without danger to human life or injury to property.

TO GET RID OF RATS.

To get clear of rats, besides using traps, cats, or dogs, try chloride of lime. It is said they never come where that is placed.

TO FLAVOR SOUPS.

Turnip peel washed clean and tied in a knot imparts a flavor to soups. Celery leaves and ends serve the same purpose.

INK SPOTS ON FINGERS.

Ink is removed from the fingers in a very simple manner. Wet the fingers and then rub the phosphorus end of a match on the spot. Wipe the fingers and renew the action until the spot has disappeared.

RELEASING ICE CREAM OR JELLY FROM MOULDS.

Fold a hot cloth around the mould and jelly or ices will leave without sticking.

CLEANING PAINT.

Put two ounces of soda in a quart of hot water, and wash with it, rinsing the paint off with pure water.

"ROYAL HOUSEHOLD" is two flours in one. It makes just as fine pastry as it does bread—and the best of both.

122

TABLE OF WEIGHTS AND MEASURES.

4 teaspoons of a liquid equal 1 tablespoon.
4 tablespoons of a liquid equal ½ gill or ¼ cup.
½ cup equals 1 gill.
2 gills equal 1 cup.
2 cups equal 1 pint.
2 pints (4 cups) equal 1 quart.
4 cups or flour equal 1 pound or 1 quart.
2 cups of butter, solid, equal 1 pound.
½ cup of butter, solid, equals ¼ pound, 4 ounces.
2 cups of granulated sugar equal 1 pound.
2½ cups of powdered sugar equal 1 pound.
1 pint of milk or water equals 1 pound.
1 pint of chopped meat equals 1 pound.
10 eggs, shelled equal 1 pound.
8 eggs with shells equal 1 pound.
2 tablespoons of butter equal 1 ounce.
2 tablespoons of granulated sugar equal 1 ounce.
4 tablespoons of flour equal 1 ounce.
4 tablespoons of coffee equal 1 ounce.
1 tablespoon of liquid equals ½ ounce.
4 tablespoons of butter equal 2 ounces or ¼ cup.

All measurements are level unless otherwise stated in the recipe.

COMPARATIVE STRENGTH OF BAKING POWDER AND CREAM TARTAR.

In cases where it is preferable to use baking powder in place of cream tartar and soda or visa-versa, use more of the baking powder, than total amount of cream tartar and soda.

EXAMPLE.—If directions called for 2 teaspoons cream tartar, and 1 teaspoon soda, use 4 teaspoons baking powder.

TIME FOR BAKING

Beans, 8 to 10 hours.

Beef, sirloin, rare, per lb., 8 to 10 minutes.

Beef, sirloin, well done, per pound, 12 to 15 minutes.

Beef, rolled rib or rump, per pound 12 to 15 minutes.

Beef, long or short fillet, 20 to 30 minutes.

Bread, brick loaf, 40 to 60 minutes.

Biscuit, 10 to 20 minutes.

Cake, plain, 20 to 40 minutes.

Cake, sponge, 45 to 60 minutes.

Chickens, 3 to 4 pound weight, 1 to 1½ hours.

Cookies, 10 to 15 minutes.

Custards, 15 to 20 minutes.

Duck, tame, 40 to 60 minutes.

Fish, 6 to 8 lbs., 1 hour.

Gingerbread, 20 to 30 minutes.

Graham Gems, 30 minutes.

Lamb, well done, per lb., 15 minutes.

Mutton, rare, per pound, 10 minutes.

Mutton, well done, per pound, 15 minutes.

Pie crust, 30 to 40 minutes.

Pork, well done, per pound, 30 minutes.

Potatoes, 30 to 45 minutes.

Pudding, bread, rice and tapioca, 1 hour.

Pudding, plum, 2 to 3 hours.

Rolls, 10 to 15 minutes.

Turkey, 10 pounds, 3 hours.

Veal, well done, per pound, 20 minutes.

A china egg may fool even the hen, but it makes a mighty poor omelette. Because a flour is said to be "just as good as ROYAL HOUSEHOLD" is a mighty poor reason for using it.

CONTENTS

CONTENTS

Page

Page

CONTENTS

NOTE

We cannot be responsible for Recipes, if other Flour than Ogilvie's Royal Household is used . . . .